ENGLISH

FOR INTERNATIONAL

NEGOTIATIONS

A CROSS-CULTURAL
CASE STUDY APPROACH

D1561131

ENGLISH

FOR INTERNATIONAL

NEGOTIATIONS

A CROSS-CULTURAL
CASE STUDY APPROACH

Drew Rodgers

Norwegian School of Management

CAMBRIDGE
UNIVERSITY PRESS

PUBLISHED BY THE PRESS SYNDICATE OF THE UNIVERSITY OF CAMBRIDGE
The Pitt Building, Trumpington Street, Cambridge CB2 1RP, United Kingdom

CAMBRIDGE UNIVERSITY PRESS
The Edinburgh Building, Cambridge CB2 2RU, UK   http://www.cup.cam.ac.uk
40 West 20th Street, New York, NY 10011-4211, USA   http://www.cup.org
10 Stamford Road, Oakleigh, Melbourne 3166, Australia

© Cambridge University Press 1998

This book is in copyright. Subject to statutory exception
and to the provisions of relevant collective licensing agreements,
no reproduction of any part may take place without
the written permission of Cambridge University Press.

First published by St. Martin's Press, Inc. 1997
Reprinted in 1999

Printed in the United States of America

Library of Congress Cataloging-in-Publication Data Available

ISBN 0-521-65749-0 Student's Book
ISBN 0-521-65748-2 Instructor's Manual

The case studies included in this book are entirely fictional and should not be read as describing
any actual persons or events. The inclusion of photographs of persons or events is not intended
to suggest that the case studies are about the persons or events depicted in the photographs.

Photo Credits
Page 21: Courtesy of Vingreiser, Norway; *Page 36:* Inger Margrethe Holter; *Page 50:* Svein
Olsen; *Page 58:* Dario Lopez-Mills/AP/Wide World Photos; *Page 67:* Courtesy of Felicia Røkaas;
Page 77: Courtesy of Vingreiser, Norway; *Page 89:* Susan Walsh/AP/Wide World Photos; *Page 98:*
Raghu Rai/Magnum; *Page 109:* Kenneth Murray/Photo Researchers; *Page 118:* Courtesy of the
Norwegian School of Management

SL22222 Client: Cambridge PO No.: 65749-0 Mac: Pathfinder 12/11/98 Proof 1 Galley 1
Size/Font: 7 & 8/10 Garamond book File: Rodgers

CONTENTS

CASE 9

KENJI MOTORS AND THE AMERICAN AUTO CORPORATION:

CASE 10

GROUP PRESENTATION:

PREFACE

AUDIENCE

This book is geared to students at an advanced-intermediate to advanced level. It employs the case study method, which is based on the approach used in programs at Harvard Business School and other major schools of business. The approach develops communicative competence by putting the students in the center of the action where they can use language actively and practice communication skills, while at the same time learn the fundamentals of negotiation and develop an awareness of different cultures' approach to negotiations.

The role of the teacher becomes that of negotiations coach, facilitator, reference person, and provider of feedback and the classroom becomes a workshop in communication and language skills and cross-cultural awareness development. After the cases are introduced, much of the class time is spent in group work. Students prepare their roles, while the teacher aids this preparation by providing language input and by coaching the students in negotiation strategies. The students will often ask for vocabulary and structures which they will use immediately and thus will internalize better than in rote memorization. The facilitator role helps to create a *dynamic partnership* in learning between the teacher and the students that greatly enhances the learning experience. In the *active approach to learning* fostered by this method, students will achieve *communicative competence* in English more efficiently.

Think about the traditional teacher-centered method where the teacher is the hub and all communication goes through him or her. Learning a language and communication skills requires active participation, and if only one student can speak at a time, how much learning can be accomplished? However, with the case study method, students are allowed to communicate in their individual groups, thereby multiplying the opportunities to produce language and to be corrected, as well as to practice communication and negotiation skills.

The case study method allows students to expand their repertoire of communication skills by requiring them to develop presentation, team working, networking, and critical/analytical problem-solving skills, all of which are required in a modern business context characterized by a task force or team approach. Furthermore, it helps them become sensitive negotiators.

This method does not exclude teacher-centered activities. These are integrated when defining and clarifying the cases, working on grammar and vocabulary, and coaching the students in negotiation skills. However, once completed, the students should be allowed to communicate freely.

For those with no previous experience in the case study method, rest assured that it is one of the easiest methods to use, once the proper mind-set is adopted. This mind-set requires ceding center stage to the students and assuming a support role. The teacher's role focuses on providing the students with vocabulary, grammatical structures, and content feedback, as well as helping them become sensitive negotiators.

OVERVIEW AND ORGANIZATION

The book is divided into cases representing various types of negotiation (contract, compensation, two party, multiparty) and fields of business (finance, tourism, and industry). The cases are arranged in a pedagogical order which is explained in the Instructor's Manual.

Each case is a complete unit and is pedagogically segmented to provide a logical progression in the solving of the case. Each case consists of

1. Discussion questions to help the students consider general aspects of the case
2. A cultural background section to explain cultural factors bearing on the two teams' negotiating style
3. A description of the situation underlying the case
4. Roles to be played and problems to be solved
5. Linguistic support
6. Written and oral assignments relevant to the case.

In addition to the cases, five appendices are included:

Appendix 1: Business Writing provides models for letters, reports, and memos, and discussions of proper tone and style, and audience-centered communication to aid the student in completing the written assignments in each case.

Appendix 2: Telephone English is designed to help students develop telephone-related skills and language as well as accepted telephone etiquette.

Appendix 3: Negotiations Worksheet

Appendix 4: Position Presentation Worksheet

Appendix 5: A Compilation of Language Exercises are additional exercises to the exercises in each individual case.

An Instructor's Manual accompanies this text. It provides an in-depth explanation of the rationale behind the case study method, the teacher's and students' roles, the progression from introduction to writing assignment in the cases, tips relevant to teaching each individual case, and secret position papers for the individual teams to help them prepare for the negotiation. Thus, no previous experience in using the case study method is necessary to use this book successfully.

Acknowledgements

I would like to thank the following reviewers for their insights and suggestions:

Christine Uber Grosse, American School of International Management
Beth Brooks Cattel, University of California, Berkeley, extension
Eva Stachniak, Sheridan College
Steven Darian, Rutgers University
Dr. Rosemary Khoo, FEAMEO Regional Language Centre
Emily Catherine Day, Eastern Michigan University
Miguel Parmentie-Kennedy, I.C.A.D.E.

Special thanks to Editor Tina B. Carver and to Karen George for their excellent cooperation and efficiency.

INTRODUCTION

TO THE STUDENT

You are the key to the success of the teaching method behind this book. You will be the focus of this method because it depends on your ability to play the roles assigned you. Although this book is geared to ESP-Business Negotiations courses, the method will allow you to learn more than just English. You will learn many skills that are valuable in the business world:

1. How to make public presentations
2. How to actively share your knowledge of the business world so as to improve your marketability as a candidate for future jobs (networking)
3. How to work in teams
4. How to find necessary information
5. How to deal with foreign cultures, their values and ways of doing business and negotiating
6. How to participate actively in problem-solving activities
7. How to argue and negotiate effectively

To achieve these goals, you will have to follow three basic rules:

1. *Be active* in all group and class work. You have to participate to learn.
2. *Speak only English* in class except when you do not know a word and ask a fellow student or the teacher for a translation.
3. *Come to class prepared.* Remember, the role playing on which this method is based depends on your preparedness and ability to play the roles assigned to you.

If you follow these three basic rules, you will not only learn English, but you will develop the seven valuable business skills mentioned, thereby greatly improving your chances in a competitive job market.

There are no right answers. Each group will have to work out its own solutions and present them in the role plays. You will all be able to solve problems, use your communication skills to present your solutions, and help each other by sharing your ideas. This approach is not only an excellent way to learn language and communication skills, but it is also fun. Good luck!

TO THE INSTRUCTOR

This book is geared to students with advanced-intermediate to advanced proficiency in English and is intended for business people and students of business both in non-English speaking countries and at schools of business in English-speaking countries. An Instructor's Manual is available. It has an introduction on how to teach with the case study method in general and provides detailed information on how to teach each case. The Instructor's Manual gives advice on teaching vocabulary and grammar, presents the teaching sequence for the cases (how much time to devote to each part of the cases), and gives answer keys for the language exercises, and contains secret position papers for the teams. *It is a must.*

The sequence of negotiations: Each case consists of all or part of the following segments:

- Original contact via letter or telephone
- Arranging a meeting, including decisions regarding place and time
- Preparation for the negotiations
- Preparing for the negotiations by filling out the Negotiations and Position Presentation Worksheets (see Appendices 3 and 4)
- The host team prepares the setting and agenda
- The negotiations
- Socializing (including introductions) and gift exchange (if appropriate); explanation of the agenda by the host team and information about where and when meetings and social activities will take place
- Negotiations and breaks (any breaks will be considered as a continuation of the negotiations)
- Oral documentation of what was decided as the negotiations proceed
- Written documentation of the agreement
- The team assigned the responsibility for documenting the outcome of the negotiations will summarize the results and send them in the form of a letter to the other team, who will write a letter either confirming or questioning the stated results.

An overview of case levels follows on page xvi.

OVERVIEW OF CASE LEVELS

Case 1: Sun and Fun Tours vs. Hotel de la Playa: A Compensation for Breach of Agreement—*Advanced-Intermediate*

Case 2: Sansung Sporting Goods Seeks a Scandinavian Distributor: An Agency Agreement—*Advanced-Intermediate*

Case 3: Acme Water Pumps and the Nigerian Government: A Sales Contract—*Advanced-Intermediate*

Case 4: American Auto Corporation vs. the Mexican Auto Workers' Union: Wage and Working Conditions Negotiations—*Advanced-Intermediate*

Case 5: Hydra Tech and Bertoni Shipping: Product Presentation and a Sales Contract—*Advanced-Intermediate*

Case 6: Tourism Comes to Zanir: Development of a Tourist Resort—*Advanced*

Case 7: Smirnov Goes to Paris St. Germain: A Player's Contract—*Advanced*

Case 8: Chemi Suisse vs. the State of India: A Catastrophe and Claims for Compensation—*Advanced*

Case 9: Kenji Motors and the American Auto Corporation: A Joint Venture—*Advanced*

Case 10: Group Presentation: An Open-Ended Case—*Advanced*

CHAPTER 1

THE ART
OF NEGOTIATING

The art of negotiating involves finding a balance between achieving the best possible result, while at the same time establishing a *mutually beneficial* working relationship with your *counterparts*. (Definitions of all words in *italics* are given in a vocabulary list at the end of this chapter.) Much negotiation literature, including the best-seller book *Getting to Yes*, emphasizes inventing *options* for *mutual gain* rather than negotiating on a win-lose basis. The former tries to expand the pie by discovering new options, while the latter sees negotiations as a fixed pie where the more one side wins, the more the other side loses. The idea behind the "Getting to Yes" *approach* is that it is unproductive to lock yourself into a fixed position because that will prevent you from finding *alternatives* that will be mutually beneficial. One example is when a major American soft drink producer was attempting a *market penetration* in the former Soviet Union. One of the *major* problems was the means of payment. The soft drink producer wanted payment in dollars, but the Soviets did not want to exhaust their limited dollar reserves. The whole deal could have fallen apart if both sides had locked themselves into their *predetermined* positions and simply repeated the importance of the other side accepting it. What they did instead was to seek out alternative solutions to satisfy *mutual* needs. You will be asked to analyze this case and find a solution in the exercise at the end of this chapter.

Another problem with fixed positions and a win-lose orientation is that most business relations involve long-term cooperation. Naturally, you want to achieve the best possible result for your company, but at the same time you do not want to poison the ongoing business relationship on which your future success depends. Negotiations are a case of give and take, and good negotiators are sensitive to the *priorities* and musts of the other side. Beating the other side into submission, even though it may give you a sense of victory, is certainly not the way to establish the *atmosphere* of mutual understanding necessary for an ongoing business relationship.

Thus, in negotiating you should consider the following:

Establish Interests and Not Positions

As suggested, emphasizing interests allows negotiators to arrive at mutually satisfying solutions that will become the basis for a positive ongoing business relationship. Establishing interests is a two-part process. First, you must clearly establish your interests; second, you must *strive* to understand your counterparts' interests. You should try to put yourself in the others' shoes and let them know that you have tried to understand their position. For example, in the case "Tourism Comes to Zanir," the Abenteuer Urlaub team could establish an understanding of the interests involved by stating first that they see Zanir as an attractive tourist destination because of its unspoiled nature and beautiful beaches, which would be highly attractive to the German tourists and thus profitable for both parties. They could go on by saying that they understand the Zanirian authorities' *concerns* about economic development and the protection of their cultural traditions. So as not to sound as if they are *presupposing* the Zanirian position, they could preface their statements by "as we understand it" or "correct us if we are wrong."

Do Not Underestimate the Importance of Socializing and Protocol

Almost every case will begin with some socializing before sitting down at the negotiating table. This can involve the exchange of business cards and "gifts" and conversation with compliments, expectations for a mutually beneficial relationship, and sharing of interests and hobbies—for example, your golf handicap and favorite courses—anything to create a relationship. You will also want to establish a sense of mutual respect and, when important to the culture of your counterparts, respect for senior members. The socializing will be followed by the host team's leader seating the delegations and officially presenting the members of his or her team, including their titles. The visiting delegation's leader will then present his or her team in the same way. All members will have name cards with their titles in front of them.

Breaks in the negotiations will also provide an opportunity for socializing and for *sounding out* individual members concerning their feelings about issues. Each team must carefully determine how much *leeway* its individual members have in discussing positions outside the negotiation room.

Take the Other Side's Position Seriously

As an extension of focusing on interests and not positions, do not just look at the other side's position as something to be *brushed aside* on your way to victory. Put yourself in their shoes and try to understand why they want what they want.

This will help you understand interests and not focus on positions, which in turn will help you arrive at creative alternative solutions. For example, in the Zanir case, the German team must be sensitive not only to African history but to present needs. In order to understand Zanirians' skepticism to tourist development, they must understand what centuries of colonialism have done to Zanirian *perception* of Europeans' intentions. The Zanirians could easily view their German counterparts as there to *exploit* Zanir's natural resources as has historically been the case in European-African relations. Thus, the Germans must emphasize that they understand the Zanirians' need for economic development and create a sense that this project can result in mutual gain. Naturally, this may weaken the German position, but failing to understand the Zanirians' needs may spoil the entire deal.

Depersonalize and Focus on Substance

Establishing *good chemistry* among negotiators is important since you will be involved in a long-term relationship where problems will arise. Thus, you have to establish a good working relationship in order to have a basis for dealing with the *eventual* problems. However, at the same time, you must avoid taking disagreements personally. You must focus on the problem and not conclude that your counterpart is unfair, unreasonable, or unreliable. It is easy to resort to such attacks when negotiations become *deadlocked* or problems arise, but emotional responses and personal attacks will destroy a working relationship faster than anything. Attack the problem and not your counterpart. Remember, both sides have their perception of the problem, their interests, and usually a mutual interest in solving the problem.

Listen and Observe Actively

Entering negotiations with a *preconceived* notion of the "only right outcome" and a fixed position will prevent you from listening to and observing your counterparts. They will be sending you verbal and non-verbal signals constantly, and you must perceive them and acknowledge them if you are to arrive at a mutually satisfying agreement. Thus, expressions such as, "As I understand your position," or "If I understand you correctly" help you to ensure that you have understood your counterparts' position as well as sending them a message that you are honestly trying to understand their position and take it into consideration. This helps establish a sense of mutuality which is the basis of negotiations geared at reaching a satisfying agreement.

Furthermore, listening can help you pick up signals as to how far your counterparts are willing to go to meet you. A classic case is that of a soft drink producer who wanted to break into a restaurant chain dominated by the "number l" producer. The negotiating team went in trying to be accepted along with the existing supplier and couldn't understand why they were getting nowhere until one of the team members picked up a hint that the restaurant chain was dissatisfied with the present supplier and was willing to give the entire contract to the new supplier. Naturally, this is an extreme case, but awareness of your counterparts' communication, both verbal and non-verbal, is an important part of negotiations. This is extremely important in international negotiations, where verbal and non-verbal signs differ. You must not only be aware of these signs, but capable of interpreting them in their context. For example, if an American says, "that might be difficult," it means that something still might be worked out. However, if a Japanese negotiator says the same thing, it is most likely a polite way of saving face while *rejecting* a proposal. With non-verbal communication, otherwise known as body language, there are further problems. In-high context cultures (cultures where words' meanings have to be interpreted from the social context in which they are spoken and verbal communication is imprecise), body language, pauses, even grunts can be more communicative than words. This subject will be taken up in the next chapter along with the importance of understanding the culture of those with whom you are negotiating.

Periodically Summarize Agreement As You Are Going Along

In order to avoid misunderstandings that lead to two different interpretations of the final agreement, summarize what has been decided. Use sentences such as, "So far we have decided ...," or "Now let us move on to the question of ...." So as not to seem to dictate the summary of what has been decided, you can add, "As we understand it, we have arrived at the following agreement. / We have decided ...."

Establish a Feeling of Fairness by Using Objective Criteria

When resolving disputes, resort to established criteria rather than ones that simply favor your position. One means is to look at similar cases and see what criteria were used and what agreement was arrived at. Another means is to subject the case to a neutral party—an independent consultant. A third approach is to carefully examine how both sides arrived at their figures. Often this will lead to compromise, especially if one or both sides cannot *document* how they arrived at their figures. When making your proposals, present your statements in a positive way by using expressions such as: "Don't you think a fair compromise would be ...," "To reach a fair solution, we propose ...," or "We are willing to approach your position/meet you half way and propose ...." These expressions are also tactical since they suggest that your counterparts are unreasonable if they reject your position.

Document Your Position and Present It Logically

Your position will be more convincing if you have the facts to support it. Thus, use statistics, figures, and examples from similar negotiations. A position presentations worksheet is provided in Appendix 4 and should be filled out in advance of your negotiation. An example drawn from the Zanirian team's presentation in the case "Tourism Comes to Zanir" would look like this.

POSITION: We require 51 percent ownership of the project, including the cost of the hotel stay. Thus, we require that you break down the cost of the package sold in your country and transfer 51 percent of the cost of the hotel stay to us in German marks (Deutsche Marks). The calculation of the hotel stay will be determined by agreement between your accountant and ours.

DOCUMENTATION: Our neighboring country developed a similar resort project to that which you propose based on 100 percent ownership of the resort by the foreign company. Their experience shows that 90 percent of the money spent by tourists was either spent in buying the package in the company's country or spent at the hotel. Thus, the profits for the country, DM 1,000,000 per year, were not sufficient to cover the costs of the improvements in the *infrastructure* necessary for the project. Here are the figures furnished by the Sendalian Ministry of Commerce for your review. (Then you present the figures.)

CONSEQUENCES: Based on these figures, the project would result in negative cash flow for our country. You must admit that for a project to be attractive, there has to be a profit potential in it for both sides. (Note the appeal to fairness and commonly accepted good business practices.)

Establish a Positive Mind Set Before Entering the Negotiations

Do not look at your counterpart as someone who is out to cheat you or someone whom you are going to manipulate to your own advantage. Enter negotiations with a positive attitude that an agreement can be reached which will be mutually beneficial. Establish this feeling at the beginning of the negotiations by being friendly toward your counterparts. The protocol of introductions, exchanging business cards, complimenting your counterparts and their company, showing due respect for senior members, and being pleasant are all part of establishing the right tone. Do not overlook the importance of the social aspects of negotiations.

Emphasizing the mutual benefits that can be achieved early in the negotiations is also a means of expressing a positive *attitude* toward the result of the negotiations.

Emphasize the Positive

As a follow-up to the tone established in the beginning, emphasize the progress made as you move through the negotiations and the benefits to be gained by further progress. Use phrases such as, "Good, we have made good progress on items one and two, so let's see what we can do with item three" or "Good, I think we both feel encouraged about our progress so far and we are on our way to a mutually satisfying agreement."

Know Your Limits

Before the negotiations, set your opening offer and your *resistance point*— the point you would resist going beyond. Factor into your resistance point the *concessions* you would require to move beyond that point. Finally, set your *bottom line*—the limit you are willing to go to before breaking off negotiations. When approaching that point, in a last attempt to save the negotiations, you might add: "It looks as if further negotiations seem *pointless*." In an attempt to save the negotiations, you can mention the advantages of achieving an agreement, but that any agreement must be based on mutual gain. You can emphasize your desire to achieve a satisfying agreement by saying, "We had hoped to achieve a mutually satisfying agreement and still do, but you will have to be willing to meet us half way," or something similar.

Be Prepared

Assess the balance of power and get as clear a picture as possible of how much you need what the team can offer you and what your alternatives are and how much they need you and what their alternatives are. This will require filling out the negotiations worksheet in Appendix 3. Furthermore, gain an understanding of your counterparts' culture and its impact on their approach to negotiations, which is discussed in the next chapter.

Be Aware of Tactics and Tricks

In spite of everything that has been said about the importance of achieving a mutually satisfying agreement, both sides wish to achieve the best possible agreement for themselves. Negotiating is a *tightrope act* between mutuality and individual gain. Thus, tactics and even tricks will be involved. If your counterparts feel that you are vulnerable to their tactics or tricks, they will naturally be tempted to use them. What you must do is to be aware of the kinds of tactics and tricks they may use. You can even confront them with, "You're not using the "good cop, bad cop" on us, are you?" I thought we were going to try to reach a mutually satisfying agreement." You appeal to fairness, while at the same time showing them that you know what tactic they are trying. In doing this at the *outset,* your counterparts will be less tempted to try to manipulate you, and negotiations can move on to the next level where mutually satisfying solutions can be achieved. The following section discusses some important considerations and some tricks to be aware of.

HOME FIELD ADVANTAGE: There are definite advantages with playing on your home field. You have your own support network, both social and business, while your visitors are far from friends, family, and business support. Staying in hotels and dealing with foreign cultures can *wear them out* to the point that they will more readily accept a deal just to get back to the comforts of their environment.

STALLING: If your counterparts know that you have a return flight or a deadline, they can wait you out, forcing you to accept their terms due to the deadline. Make it quite clear that you have all the time in the world, even if you do not.

WEARING YOU OUT: Pretending to be social, the host team can provide many social activities to wear you out and dull your senses. Negotiating is a demanding activity requiring complete alertness. You need to be rested and alert, so do not let yourself be exhausted to the point where you are on the defensive. Simply decline those invitations that prevent you from staying rested and alert.

UNFAVORABLE POSITIONING: Positioning around the negotiating table may sound like a simple matter, but it can be part of psychological warfare. For example, if your hosts know that the sun will shine in your faces at 3:00 PM just about the time that you are reaching an important decision, they may place you on a certain side of the table. You must either be aware of this possibility and mention it in the beginning or politely ask to be moved when the sun starts shining in your face.

MISREPRESENTING FACTS: "How to lie with statistics" is a well-known phrase. If you doubt the accuracy of your counterparts' facts or figures, you may ask them to document them—that is show how they arrived at them, including the source of their information. If they have obviously invented the facts or figures, your questioning may be enough to have them revise them. If necessary, you can have an independent consultant/assessor go over figures, especially in *assessing* the value of something. Another approach is to hire your own assessor and use those figures as a point of departure in negotiating the true value of the thing in question.

TWO BITES OF THE APPLE: This is a question of the *authority* of your counterparts to conclude a deal. You must establish early that the people with whom you are dealing have final authority to sign an eventual contract. Otherwise they might use the "two bites of the apple" approach, which means that after you have reached an agreement and *exposed* your position, they say that they have to submit the proposal to their boss for final approval. The boss then accepts those parts of the contract that are favorable for him or her and subjects the remainder to further negotiation.

GOOD COP, BAD COP: A negotiating team is divided into two groups—the good cop and bad cop. In this approach, taken from police *interrogation,* the bad cop players take a very hard-line approach and try to wear you down. After hammering at you, a break is taken where the "good cops" talk to you, try to flatter your ego, and suggest a slightly moderated position, but one that you would not normally accept if you had not been so badly battered by the "bad cops." The "good cops" seem friendly, considerate, and reasonable in comparison to the "bad cops," and they get you to go along with an unfavorable compromise. The best way to avoid this is simply not to allow yourself to judge the situation relative to the "bad cop," but to maintain your original goals.

These are just a few examples of important considerations and standard tricks used in negotiations. Your job is not to be tricked, and the best way is simply to confront the opposing side. While showing that you understand the tactic, you also establish yourself as being both professional and ethical and can then demand that you move on to "real" negotiations based on mutuality, honesty, and fairness.

MAKING THREATS: Typical threats are "Accept this or I'll buy from company X" or "We'll take you to court." When *confronted* by such threats, one has to determine the *likelihood* of them being carried out. Ways of assessing this likelihood are (1) the seniority of the person making the threat—the higher up in the organization, the more power he or she has and the greater the likelihood, (2) past performance—has this person carried out threats before, and (3) what this person and company stand to lose if the threat is carried out and the question of who needs whom more—the balance of power discussed in the Negotiations Worksheet in Appendix 3.

FISHING: Overstating a demand to discover a counterpart's reaction. If the reaction is strong, including body language (crossing of arms, angry expression), then the resistance on that point will be strong. This is a way of determining where your counterparts will be less flexible (their high-priority items) and where they are likely to make concessions and you can push for an *optimal* result. If someone tries this tactic on you, here are various possible responses:

> ***Confrontational.*** "You can't be serious." *(Followed by silence. Often used to attack what is considered to be a bluff.)*
>
> ***Polite rejection.*** "I'm afraid we cannot consider that a reasonable offer." *(Followed by silence.)*
>
> ***Treating it as a misunderstanding.*** "Perhaps there is a misunder–standing here. Could you explain your position?" *(This forces your counterparts to expose their position.)*

STANDARD CONTRACT: Your counterpart presents the proposal as "This is a standard contract for the industry." You can counter by saying that the contract, if it is unfavorable, is unlike the contracts you have dealt with in all your other negotiations.

PLEASE REPEAT THAT, AS I AM NOT SURE I UNDERSTAND: A tactic used when a person wants to get a counterpart to reveal *inconsistencies* which can be used against her or him. The more a person speaks, the more likely he will reveal the real motives, thus exposing and weakening that bargaining position. This also gives you more time to consider a response.

NO INITIAL COMPROMISE: Typical for Western negotiators is to agree on areas where agreement can be reached with limited concessions and then negotiate questions where the gap in the two positions is wider. However, some negotiating styles are based on no initial compromise on any point, even when taking an extreme position. The point is to wear down one's counterparts and make them compromise more than they normally would.

VOCABULARY

alternative, *n.* Other possible solution

approach, *n.* A way of doing something

to assess, *v.* To determine the value of something

atmosphere, *n.* The mood or feeling

attitude *n.* The way one feels or thinks about something

authority, *n.* The power to make a decision

to be brushed aside, *v.* To be ignored

concern, *n.* Interest or worry

to confront, *v.* To be faced with directly (this can be done in an aggressive manner)

counterpart, *n.* Member of the opposing team

deadlocked, *adj.* When negotiations cannot proceed because both sides are unwilling to compromise

to document, *v.* To supply evidence

eventual, *adj.* Something that may happen in the future

to exploit, *v.* To use for one's benefit or profit (this can be done at the expense of someone else)

to expose, *v.* To make known, to reveal

good chemistry, *n.* A good relation or feeling toward another person

imprecise, *adj.* Not clear

inconsistency, *n.* Idea that do not follow logically

infrastructure, *n.* The basic foundation of society such as communication systems, roads, water, electricity

initial, *adj.* The first, the beginning

interrogation, *n.* Questioning

leeway, *n.* A certain freedom before reaching limits or restrictions

likelihood, *n.* The probability that something will happen

major, *adj.* The main or most important

market penetration, *n.* Entering a new market with a product

to misrepresent facts, *v.* To present facts which are not correct

must, *n.* Important demand that you must get if you are going to accept an agreement

mutual, *adj.* Something done or felt by each side toward the other

mutual gain, *n.* Where both sides profit

mutually beneficial, *adj.* Good for both sides

optimal, *adj.* The best possible

option, *n.* Choice

outset, *n.* The beginning

perception, *n.* The way someone sees or regards something

pointless, *adj.* There is no reason (in this case to continue the negotiations)

preconceived, *adj.* Determined in advance

predetermined, *adj.* Determined in advance

to presuppose, *v.* To guess in advance

priority, *n.* How you rate something in terms of its importance (high priority, low priority)

to reject, *v.* To say no (to something)

to sound out, *v.* To ask questions to get an idea as to a person's feelings about a certain issue

to strive, *v.* To attempt

tightrope act, *n.* A difficult balance

to wear someone out, *v.* To tire out, exhaust someone; to cause someone to become tired/exhausted

EXERCISES

In groups, discuss the following situations and questions and be ready to present your answers to the class.

1. In the first paragraph in this chapter, the following case was presented:

   When a major American soft drink producer was attempting a market penetration in the former Soviet Union, one of the major problems was the means of payment. The soft drink producer wanted payment in dollars, but the Soviets did not want to exhaust their limited dollar reserves. The whole deal could have fallen apart if both sides had locked themselves into their predetermined positions and simply repeated the importance of the other side accepting it. What they did instead was to seek out alternative solutions to satisfy mutual needs.

   In groups, discuss this case and determine the following:
   a. What would have happened if both sides had dug themselves into their positions?
   b. What were their common interests?
   c. Find a solution which satisfies both side's common interests.

Positions	Americans	Soviets
Interests		
Your solution		

2. Social activities are important in the negotiating process. What social activities would you arrange with members of a team with which you are negotiating to create a good relationship? Describe the nature of the negotiations, the type of activities, and when and where you would hold them.

3. Listening actively and showing that you are aware of the other side's position and take it seriously are important parts of negotiating. List four phrases that you might use to show these skills. Two are given in the text, but you must develop two more.

4. How can you establish a positive atmosphere at the beginning of a negotiation?

5. List three tactics which might be used to manipulate you. What could you do if these were used against you?

CHAPTER 2

CULTURAL AWARENESS IN INTERNATIONAL NEGOTIATIONS

Negotiation is not just a matter of arriving at a contract—the deal. It is a complicated process that involves a number of factors, many of which are culturally determined. You must never *assume* that your counterparts from another culture think like you do. (Definitions of all words in *italics* are given in a vocabulary list at the end of this chapter. After completing this chapter, you should be familiar with looking up words in the vocabulary lists at the end of each chapter. If there are any new words in the case, check the vocabulary list for a definition.) Doing so can lead to misunderstanding, frustration, and distrust, which may sour the climate of the negotiations and even lead to *failure* to arrive at an agreement. Classic examples are (1) the question of time, (2) disagreement on the importance of protocol, and (3) conflicts arising from a deal orientation versus a relationship-establishing orientation in negotiation meetings. The question of time can create frustration and misunderstanding between a culture emphasizing *punctuality*, such as Germany, and one where punctuality is of less importance, such as in Latin cultures. German negotiators can easily interpret "Latin time" as being disrespectful if they are kept waiting. On the other hand, representatives from Latin cultures can feel that the German emphasis on punctuality is "pushy." These conflicting reactions can create an underlying tension, which could sour the atmosphere surrounding the negotiations. Disagreement on the importance of protocol between formal cultures, such as Japan, and informal cultures, such as the United States, can be equally disruptive. The Japanese culture is characterized by rituals such as bowing and the formalistic exchanging of business cards (with two hands), which shows the status of the individuals and others' acceptance of this status. The American emphasis on informality and the attempt to be on a personal first-name basis may be interpreted as disrespectful, particularly among the older and more traditional members of a Japanese delegation. This can lead to a loss of face, which is serious in Japanese culture and in most cases is *irreversible*. Finally, the goal of the negotiation process may be totally different for the two teams. U.S. negotiators are traditionally deal-oriented, and the purpose of their negotiations is to arrive at a written, binding contract. Saudi negotiators, on the other hand, are more relationship-oriented, and their goal is to form a friendship which will be the basis of a long-lasting business relationship. The standard saying is, "establish friendship and business will follow." Thus, a Saudi might regard an American push for the signed contract as a sign of distrust. Furthermore, the establishing of a relationship takes more time than many American negotiators have "budgeted." With a return ticket on a specific flight purchased, the American may push for the conclusion of negotiations, where the Saudi would like to take the extra time necessary to get to know his counterpart(s).

The purpose of this chapter, and the resulting exercise at the end of it, is to create an awareness of the possible differences in values underlying approaches to negotiations, which can lead to misunderstandings, frustration, conflicts, and failed deals. It will contain certain generalizations about the way representatives from different cultures negotiate—the culture of negotiations—which, like all generalizations, will not hold true in all cases. However, they will form a framework with which to deal with members of another culture. The *applicability* of the generalizations will vary from culture to culture. They will hold true to a greater degree with formalistic cultures, such as Japan, where there are rigid rules of behavior. They will be less accurate in individualistic cultures, such as that of the United States, where there is more individual freedom of action. Nevertheless, they should be learned so that (1) you avoid the mistake of assuming that everyone thinks and negotiates like you, and (2) you develop a sensitivity to different meanings attached to different gestures, means of expression (direct versus indirect communication), concepts of time, and so forth. Negotiation is a dialogue, and a dialogue requires an understanding of the differences associated with acts, statements, and body language. Understanding these differences will help you avoid misinterpretation, mistakes in communication, and even insults, all of which can result in failed deals.

The assignment at the end is intended as a consciousness-raising exercise to sharpen your sensitivity to other cultures' approach to negotiations. In addition, each case has a similar introductory exercise to establish the approaches of the cultures represented in the case and indicate possible areas of misunderstanding that could lead to failed negotiations. The American culture of negotiation is used as an example and compared with contrasting cultures on each point.

TIME: Negotiations should begin on time. "Time is money," and thus negotiations should not take more time than necessary. This means that American negotiators are sometimes frustrated by what they see as "Latin time" where meetings don't start promptly or the Arab tendency to want to establish friendship before negotiations can really begin. Americans are very goal-oriented, set up time schedules, and hope to conclude negotiations within those time frames. They can appear to be impatient or "pushy" (pressuring the opposite side to come to an agreement). Whereas a Chinese negotiator must convince his superior that he has fully explored the limits of his counterpart's position, an American negotiator may want to prove his efficiency by making a quick deal.

Another conflict may arise due to differing *perceptions* of time. Some cultures such as North American, British, and Germanic function under Monochronic time, which is linear and has segments which can be compartmentalized allowing people to concentrate on one thing at a time. Thus, negotiations should proceed from A to Z and not be interrupted. This is typical of American thinking. Other cultures, notably Arab, function under Polychronic time, where many things can occur at the same time. This can be a source of conflict between American and Arab negotiators because the latter allows many things to occur at the same time. For example, a telephone call or a secretary's interruption are perfectly acceptable in a Polychronic time culture, whereas they would be considered impolite and frustrating for a member of a Monochronic time culture.

CONTRACT: American look at negotiations as a means of reaching a contract and *stress* legality and the binding nature of a written document, which sets out rights and duties that can be upheld in a court of law. Other cultures look at negotiations as a means of establishing a relationship that will be the basis of future business. For Americans, a contract is the sign of closing a deal, while for some other cultures it begins a relationship. The emphasis on a binding legal document may be interpreted by other cultures as a sign of a lack of trust. They often see a contract as a general outline of the present situation, which can be *altered* if a new situation arises. Thus, for legalistic cultures, such as Western European and North American, the Oriental tendency to look at a contract as a point of departure is very frustrating. The legalist interprets changes in a contract as *breach of contract*, which can be brought to court. Many Oriental negotiators feel that if a situation changes, the agreement should change, and that the original agreement was a statement of principles that can be worked out over time if the relationship between the two sides is good.

DEAL VERSUS RELATIONSHIP: A basic source of misunderstanding is an emphasis on making a deal versus establishing a relationship. Making a deal is typical of legalistic cultures such as Western Europe and North America, whereas establishing a relationship is typical of Oriental, Latin American, and Arab cultures. Legalistic cultures try to establish an "airtight" contract that takes into consideration all *contingencies*. Members of a relationship-oriented culture realize that the world is not static and *unanticipated* changes will occur that will require the reinterpretation of the original agreement. Thus, when a Japanese businessman seeks to modify a contract, the American will likely feel that he is being cheated. Whereas the Japanese will likely feel that the American is being unreasonably rigid and distrustful. The difference in emphasis on deal versus relationship may even affect the emphasis of the negotiations. A Japanese or Chinese negotiator will likely begin with an agreement on general principles, while an American will begin with specific details.

Naturally, the emphasis on building a relationship results in a more *prolonged* negotiation period. The American impatience to close the deal might not consider the importance of establishing a sound relationship, which is *disconcerting* for representatives of relationship-oriented cultures. Failure to recognize the importance of personal relationships can undermine the basic foundation of a working relationship. It is almost *contradictory* that Americans, who are extremely social, often place so little emphasis on relationship-building in international negotiations.

PROTOCOL: Protocol concerns the importance of the formal aspects of negotiations. It includes aspects such as how to address people (first or last names), use of titles, dress, gift giving, exchange of business cards, the respect for age, the shape of the negotiating table, the placement of negotiators, *etiquette* of conducting business over a meal, and so forth. Americans are informal and have a tendency to over-look the importance of protocol, which can be interpreted as impoliteness. Protocol functions to establish a relationship, and those who overlook the importance of relationship may overlook the importance of protocol. It helps to establish respect through gift giving and business card exchange, and respect for culturally determined rules of the game. Failure to consider protocol can be interpreted as both a personal *affront* and an affront to the culture of one's counterparts. Griffin and Daggatt cite Americans' tendency to address the member of the other negotiating team who speaks English best, thus overlooking a senior member of the other team, an act which ignores seniority and implicitly shows disrespect to the point of causing loss of face. As protocol establishes a recognition of seniority among counterparts, failure to observe it can be equal to an unintentional insult. In analyzing one's counterparts, one has to decide both how important protocol is and what aspects of protocol are important.

DECISION MAKING: Approaches to decision making can be divided into individual and consensus. While in American teams the decision-making power often lies in the hands of individuals, other cultures emphasize group agreement by consensus, which naturally takes longer to achieve. Several negotiation experts have characterized the American approach as a "John Wayne" style where an individual arrives on the scene, conducts the negotiations as quickly as possible, and hopes to leave with a signed contract. This individualistic approach has several *drawbacks*. First, it is Monochronic, second, it overlooks the importance of establishing relationships, and third it can lead to excessive ego involvement. Believing that success or failure is individual, the John Wayne negotiator may take his counterparts' maneuvers personally and emotionally and lose his calm objectivity. This may lead to overreaction, which may decrease his effectiveness as a negotiator as well as poison the personal relationship between himself and his counterparts. Another problem can arise through misinterpreting the decision making process. Members of a team from an individualistic culture may conclude that the members of the negotiating team have the power to make the final decision. They will then be frustrated to find out that an agreement which they thought was final will be submitted to a larger group for approval. By then, they have stated their position, which makes them vulnerable, and the senior official of the other team can keep what is acceptable and demand that the rest be renegotiated.

An individual versus consensus approach will also *impact* on the concession process. An individual approach will allow for more flexibility in concession making. American teams tend to begin with an ideal contract and then make concessions until a compromise is reached. However, consensus-oriented teams have very little leeway in making concessions due to the difficulty they have in reaching consensus in their group. The consensus approach makes concessions difficult for the Japanese. The Russians often adopt an even more inflexible position, since they view compromise as a sign of weakness. Thus, whereas the Americans are generally willing to make concessions to reach an agreement, this approach may conflict with other cultures' negotiating styles.

In negotiating with other cultures, you must understand their negotiating approach, their attitude toward compromise, and who has the final say in accepting an agreement. Otherwise, you will be ineffective and frustrated.

CONFLICT: Conflict is not seen as necessarily negative by American negotiators and is often seen as part of the negotiating process. Emotions perhaps are more accepted than in some Asian cultures. Thus, American negotiators can appear more confrontational than some of their Asian counterparts, the Koreans being a notable exception. Certain aspects of conflict are (1) stating that you disagree, (2) making threats in terms of "if you do not accept this, we will ...," including threats of breaking off negotiations, (3) using the word "no", and (4) interrupting. This is one of the classic differences between Western European and Japanese negotiators. Japanese learn at an early age to avoid social conflict and save face. The Japanese generally do not like negotiating across a table. They *sound out* their counterparts in advance and hope to use formal meetings to present areas of agreement. The Japanese will question their counterparts in detail, not because they do not understand what is being said, but because they are looking for areas of agreement on which to build a consensus. Often adjustments in positions will be worked out outside of the negotiating room during breaks, where the Japanese negotiator will *fish* for possible agreement. The negotiator must be constantly aware of statements made outside of the negotiating room, since a suggestion may be subtly raised so as to be as easily withdrawn if not met by approval. This allows the all-important face saving. Thus, subtlety is the key. As Thayer and Weiss state, "Japanese negotiating style has been described as *awase* (to combine and adjust one thing to another). Instead of directly addressing issues, openly stating proposals and counterproposals, and generally relying on exact concepts and standardized meanings—features of an *erabi* (to select) culture such as the United States—*awase* style entails inferring the positions of the parties, assuming approximate meanings and adjusting to the situation. This style emphasizes proper form and process, even over the substance of decisions, and explains the Japanese preference for informal explorations and agreement behind-the-scenes prior to formal sessions." (Nathaniel B. Thayer and Stephen E. Weiss, "Japan: The Changing Logic of a Former Minor Power," in Hans Binnendijk, ed., *National*

Negotiating Styles, United States Department of State Publications, 1987, p. 56). Thus, those from cultures where conflict is acceptable must be extremely sensitive to subtle forms of communication by members of cultures where conflict is unacceptable. This leads us to a discussion of direct versus indirect communication.

DIRECT VERSUS INDIRECT COMMUNICATION: Direct communication involves stating exactly what you mean and expecting straight answers from others. It also involves asking questions and expecting direct answers. This is referred to as low-context communication, where facts and not the situation are important. In high-context communication, cultural constraints prevent a direct answer, and thus one has to interpret responses. For example, "no" is rarely used and can be replaced by "a bit difficult." "Yes" may not mean agreement, but simply that a request has been understood. "I'll think about it," for an American, will mean that a possibility of acceptance exists, whereas for a Japanese it might be a polite form of "no."

Eye contact is another area of difference. Americans look each other directly in the eyes, which may be considered impolite in some other countries. However, an American can interpret not looking one in the eyes, as a reason for distrust. Silence is another source of misunderstanding. Silence is perfectly acceptable in certain cultures, whereas it can be a source of embarrassment in others. It can even be used to gain concessions, where the members of one culture simply outwait the members of another who find silence *unbearable,* break down, and make a comment that leads to a concession. Often body language or grunts express more than words, and negotiators from low-context cultures must be careful about their own body language so as not to send false messages. They must also be aware of high-context culture representatives' body language to *infer* meaning where verbal communication does not exist.

WIN-WIN VERSUS WIN-LOSE: Win-win is when both sides win, while win-lose is where one side benefits at the other side's expense. The emphasis in the United States on winning may tend to push American negotiators toward win-lose strategies. Another factor is American emphasis on the individual rather than the group, which can lead to considering selfish interests higher than collective interests. Cultures that emphasize the importance of relationships will most likely emphasize win-win relationships, the idea being that a good business relationship will allow the partners to weather eventual conflicts and establish a mutually beneficial partnership. The win-win approach emphasizes finding interests that both sides have in common and developing them. The win-lose approach emphasizes making gains at the other party's expense, which creates a competitive and not a cooperative atmosphere. The win-lose approach is based on the idea of a fixed pie where one's gains result in another's losses. Win-win suggests that the pie can be expanded by looking for common interests and synergy. Needless to say, negotiations will be difficult if the two sides approach the table with conflicting strategies. Win-win negotiators must be careful that their counterparts share this approach or they will be easily exploited. It is wise to set down the win-win ground rules at the beginning if negotiations are to be profitable for both sides.

VOCABULARY

to affront, *v.*   To insult

affront, *n.*   An insult

applicability, *n.*   How much something can be used or applied

to alter *v.*   To change, modify

to assume, *v.*   To think

breach of contract, *n.*   The violation / breaking of a contract

contingency, *n.*   Unexpected occurrence

contradictory, *adj.*   Something that goes against what you have previously said

disconcerting, *adj.*   Upsetting

drawback, *n.*   Disadvantage

etiquette, *n.*   Rules of how to behave correctly

failure, *n.*   Not doing something, not being successful

to fish, *v.*   In this case, trying to discover another person's goals or tactics by raising possibilities and watching their response

to impact, *n./v.*   To influence / an influence

to infer, *v.*   To guess at or interpret

irreversible, *adj.*   Cannot be undone

leeway, *n.*   A certain freedom before reaching limits or restrictions

prolonged, *adj.*   Taking more time than expected

punctuality, *n.*   Being on time

to sound out, *v.*   To get a sense of someone's feelings or position

to stress, *v.*   To emphasize

unanticipated, *adj.*   Unexpected

unbearable, *adj.*   Something you cannot stand

EXERCISES

1. In groups, discuss the following areas of possible misunderstanding and conflicts due to cultural differences and be ready to present your answers to the class.

Each case will involve an examination of the negotiating team's negotiating style. Two groups will be selected to present the opposing team's negotiating style. After each group has presented its respective team's negotiating approach, both groups will discuss possible areas of conflict and/or misunderstanding that could create problems for the negotiations.

To familiarize yourself with this type of exercise, compare the American attitudes and approaches that have been described with those of your culture(s).

Find areas and provide examples of situations where misunderstanding, frustration, and conflicts might arise that could lead to failed negotiations. Consider the following areas:

TIME

Punctuality and Monochronic versus Polychronic time.

CONTRACT

The importance of arriving at an airtight agreement that will govern all future business relations versus viewing the contract as an outline of the present situation that can be altered if new situations arise.

DEAL VERSUS RELATIONSHIP

How important is socializing and building a relationship in your culture, and how would an emphasis on "closing the deal" as quickly and efficiently as possible be viewed?

PROTOCOL

What aspects of protocol are important in your culture, and how might they differ from American attitudes?

DECISION MAKING

How could differences in decision making in your culture and American culture lead to misunderstanding and frustration?

CONFLICT

How is conflict viewed in your culture, and does it differ from American attitudes?

DIRECT VERSUS INDIRECT COMMUNICATION

Does your culture allow direct communication? If not, what problems might arise in negotiating with a culture that does?

WIN-WIN VERSUS WIN-LOSE

How does your culture approach negotiations? If you are not sure, how would your group approach negotiations? With a win-win or a win-lose attitude? Can your approach vary from negotiation to negotiation? Give examples.

2. In groups, discuss the following situations and be prepared to present your answers to the class.

   a. A Japanese businessman gives you his business card. How do you receive it, and what do you do after you have received it?

   b. You are negotiating one-on-one with a Saudi. The telephone rings. He answers it and talks for five minutes. How are you to interpret this? Does this show disinterest in the present negotiations?

   c. You go out to dinner with a Spanish businesswoman. After you eat dinner, you start discussing business. What is her probable reaction and why?

   d. You are negotiating with a Chinese team. One of the team's members, a young person, speaks very good English, and thus you address most of your comments to him. What mistake are you probably making?

   e. You are negotiating with a Japanese team. You let it be known that you have a return flight on a certain date and state that you hope the negotiations can be completed by that date. What mistakes have you made, and how might they both damage the business relationship and be used against you?

SUN AND FUN TOURS
VS. HOTEL DE LA PLAYA

Compensation
for Breach of Agreement

CASE SUMMARY

This case involves solving a disagreement. Sun and Fun Tours has booked 50 double rooms for the winter season at Hotel de la Playa. Sun and Fun Tours received a verbal guarantee that construction work being done at the hotel would be completed by the beginning of the winter season. It will not be, and the tour company is demanding a 30 percent discount to be passed on to the guests until the work is completed.

Unforeseen events can occur which alter the situation for two parties in a contract. These events often are not taken account of in the contract unless there is a force majeure clause. Even in the case of a force majeure clause, often a conflict arises due to differing interpretations of whether the event in question is covered by the force majeure clause. In this case, there was just a verbal assurance given by the hotel that the construction work would be completed by the time the winter season began. Thus, Sun and Fun Tours has no legal justification for their demands. Nevertheless, the British emphasis on fair play and "a deal is a deal" would lead them to expect compensation for Hotel de la Playa's failure to complete their remodeling before the winter season began. The Anglo-American tradition regards the contract as binding and failure to live up to it results in court cases. Thus, the British and Americans try to write "airtight" contracts, which anticipate all eventualities and bind the parties to a strict set of rights and obligations. On the other hand, many cultures, including the Spanish, place more importance on a relationship of mutual trust as a basis of a long-lasting working relationship than enforcing contracts through legal means. They feel that in the event of unexpected circumstances the two parties should emphasize the relationship and not the contract or oral promises. In support of this approach, the bottom line in the service sector is satisfying the customer, which is in the interest of both Sun and Fun Tours and Hotel de la Playa.

Negotiations are a case of give and take, and good negotiators are sensitive to the priorities and musts of the other side. Beating the other side into submission, even though it may give a sense of victory, is certainly not the way to establish the atmosphere of mutual understanding necessary for an ongoing business relationship.

With this in mind, any preparation must take into consideration both parties' interests. **Part of your preparation for this and for all of the case negotiations in this book includes filling out the Negotiations Worksheet and the Position Presentation Worksheet. These worksheets, along with a fill-in exercise to help you, are found in Appendices 3 and 4.** What follows is a brief summary of how to fill out the worksheet.

I. Goals

Filling in the first section (goals) will be rather simple since there is only one major item to be negotiated, the 30 percent reduction. However, you must decide how much discount you (Sun and Fun Tours) demand/how much you (Hotel de la Playa) are willing to give, what concessions you are willing to make, and what you expect to get in return. In the other cases, filling out the worksheets will be more involved because the cases are more complicated. The negotiations worksheet will be repeated in Case 2, and you will be given information in the "goals" section to help you. After working on Case 2, you will be expected to fill out the worksheet on your own and will be referred to Appendix 3.

Sun and Fun Tours must determine how important getting the full 30 percent is and if they are willing to accept less compensation or other forms of compensation. How important is it to continue the business relation with Hotel de la Playa? Hotel de la Playa must determine whether they totally reject giving a full 30 percent and what the consequences might be. What other forms of compensation might be acceptable to the guests? How important is it for your hotel to continue the business relation with Sun and Fun Tours?

II. An Assessment of the Balance of Power

In spite of what was stated about the necessity of a mutually satisfying agreement, both sides will evaluate the strengths and weaknesses of the parties involved in the negotiations in order to avoid being "steamrollered" (dominated by the other side). Assessment of the balance of power will help you in determining your strategy and how much pressure you want to put on the other party (while not forgetting the importance of a mutually satisfying agreement). Some of the basic questions you have to ask is how much do we need them, what alternatives do we have, and how viable are the alternatives? Naturally, you must also ask how much do they need you.

III. Determining Your Strategy

Your strategy should be a result of your decisions on points I and II. You must determine where the bottom line is—how far you are willing to go to obtain an agreement. In addition, you must decide what you ideally hope to achieve. The final contract will fall somewhere between these two extremes, and charting them will give you a tool to evaluate the result. Maybe you will achieve a result closer to your ideal contract, and there is nothing wrong with shooting for an ideal result, as long as your goals do not appear unreasonable and you do not maintain an inflexible position.

Determine your opening position and the mood you hope to create. As mentioned in the worksheet, there are degrees of positions from hard-line to softer stances. Remember, however, this opening position will determine the atmosphere for the rest of the negotiations. So choose it with care. Preconditions are usually associated with a hard-line stance, so you must be sure that these conditions are an absolute must.

Determine what issues you want to negotiate first. This will help set the tone. If you take the low-priority issues first, you will create a tone of flexibility and good faith. You may be able to create a tone of flexibility on both sides to make it easier for you to get what you want on the must items later. Your strategy here would be to suggest that you have shown good faith and now it is their turn. On the other hand, starting with the "musts" will let you know early what the other side's position is on those items most important to you. Remember, the sensitive negotiator will constantly be listening for clues as to the other side's position and priorities. Starting with your "musts" may give you necessary clues as to their position. If you don't meet resistance, go for the maximum, and once you have attained what you want, you can be flexible on some of the other items to "sweeten the pot," thus creating an atmosphere of mutual satisfaction.

In an attempt to gain insight into the other side's position you might "go fishing" just to see what bait interests your counterparts. Once you see what interests them, you may be able to formulate a clear picture of their strategy. For example, if you are negotiating a contract for a product, you will want to know if price, after-sale service, delivery schedules, warrantees, and the like are important and in which order. Thus, you can generally talk about these items and see what seems to evoke the most interest.

The above is hardly an exhaustive study of negotiation strategy, and you should study the subject in more detail and discuss your experiences and strategies. However, this should give you enough information to solve the case. So fill out the negotiations worksheet, determine your strategy, and be sensitive to possible clues during the negotiations.

CULTURAL BACKGROUND

Two groups will be selected by the teacher to present an analysis of the two cultures of negotiations in this case—England and Spain—along the lines discussed in Chapter 2 on cross-cultural negotiations, such as (1) differing concepts of time, (2) the purpose of negotiations—establishing an airtight contract influenced by the thinking that "a deal is a deal" versus establishing a working relationship which will help both parties meet unforeseen events [extremely important in this case], (3) approaches to decision making, and (4) the value and importance of protocol and ceremony, and so forth. After each group has presented its culture, both teams will conclude by pointing out areas where, due to differences in the two cultures of negotiation, misunderstanding, frustration, and conflicts might occur.

QUESTIONS FOR DISCUSSION

1. Would you say that the point of departure for this negotiation is win-win or win-lose? Why?
2. Will the Hotel de la Playa team have any advantages in holding the negotiations on their home ground? If so, what are these advantages and how can they be exploited?

CASE

Sun and Fun Tours contracted 50 double rooms at the three star Hotel de la Playa for the winter season. When the contract was signed, the hotel gave a verbal guarantee that construction, which was in progress, would be completed on the new wing where the 50 rooms were located.

However, inclement weather and a strike delayed construction so that the wing could not be completed until two months into the winter season. The construction will not prevent guests from staying at the hotel, but there will be some construction noise, such as, hammering and electric saws. Sun and Fun Tours knows from previous experience that guests are often bothered by early morning construction noise and they demand refunds or a reduction in rates due to the inconvenience. Hotel de la Playa is a hotel, which emphasizes night life and has discos and bars. Sun and Fun Tours has booked young couples and singles, who will be quite disturbed by early morning construction noise. Thus, they made a request to Hotel de la Playa for the guests to be relocated at the chain's five star hotel at no extra cost, but this hotel was fully booked. As that alternative was not possible, Sun and Fun Tours is requesting a 30 percent reduction for the period until the hotel wing is completed. In this event, Sun and Fun Tours plans to inform their customers of the problem and offer to pass the 30 percent reduction on to them.

When confronted with Sun and Fun Tours' demands, the management of Hotel de la Playa claimed force majeure and reminded Sun and Fun Tours that the contract contained no terms of compensation if the construction was not completed on schedule. They feel that the cause of the problem was beyond their control and that they are not legally responsible and should not have to compensate for any problems the delay may cause. They further add that the rooms are completed and perfectly habitable. They have promised to limit construction time to the period 9 AM to 5 PM. However, Sun and Fun Tours is skeptical about the management's ability to deliver on this promise and knows from previous experience that many of the guests like to sleep late.

Sun and Fun Tours has suggested that they will consider canceling the contract altogether, which at this late date (one month before the season starts) would make it difficult to fill the rooms. Hotel de la Playa countered by stating that they would keep the 30 percent advance payment. Both sides have strengths on which they can draw in the negotiations. Sun and Fun Tours books 20 percent of the rooms in Hotel de la Playa through four months of the winter season. It would create some extra expense for the hotel if they had to find new tour operators for the next season. Hotel de la Playa caters to young English tourists, and if the word got out that Sun and Fun Tours had pulled out due to their dissatisfaction, it might be difficult to get another English tour operator to take over the 50 rooms. Furthermore, the emphasis on the "sun and fun" profile of the hotel limits the possibilities for Hotel de la Playa to fill the vacant rooms with other segments such as families or pensioners.

On the other hand, Hotel de la Playa is extremely popular with the sun and fun set and is always the first hotel to be booked. Thus, Sun and Fun Tours adds 10 percent to the normal full package price (transportation, hotel, and half pension) for reservations at Hotel de la Playa. The combination of the site, right on the beach, and the popular discos in the hotel, plus the hotel management's tolerance of noise have created an excellent reputation for the hotel among Sun and Fun Tours' clientele. Most of the bookings are repeat bookings a year in advance. Sun and Fun Tours have had a 98 percent booking rate over the last five years with their allotment at Hotel de la Playa, which is by far the highest rating for all of Sun and Fun Tours' allotment-based contracts. In addition, the contract is on an allotment basis, which means that Sun and Fun Tours has the responsibility to fill the rooms or bear the losses if they remain empty, which is a favorable situation for Hotel de la Playa. Finally, Sun and Fun Tours would have to cancel half of the bookings due to the difficulty of finding accommodations at this late date.

The main item to be negotiated is the 30 percent price reduction. However, other items on the agenda below are, (second in priority) some other possible means of compensation if the full 30 percent is not granted (the Hotel de la Playa team has placed this on the agenda suggesting that they are not willing to give a full 30 percent or perhaps no discount at all). The last item concerns the renewal of the contract and its length if a satisfactory agreement is reached. The Sun and Fun Tours team has seen the agenda and asked for another item to be placed as number 3 on it, a guarantee that work will be limited to the hours between 9 AM and 5 PM with compensation to be negotiated if the guarantee is broken. In order to avoid an unfortunate situation for both parties, they have decided to meet and try to negotiate a settlement.

Select groups to play both sides in the negotiations and try to negotiate a mutually satisfying settlement.

The Case Sequence

1. WRITTEN COMMUNICATION: This case will begin with communication between representatives of the two parties concerned. The manager of Hotel de la Playa, Raphael Fuentes, will write a letter to the tour manager in charge of the booking, Mrs. Margaret Smith, explaining the situation, including that there will be construction noise such as electric saws and hammering in the hallways. The duration of construction should be through the first two months of the winter season and will be limited to 9:00 AM to 5:00 PM. Naturally, Mr. Fuentes will express his regrets and say that he will do everything in his power to limit the impact on the guests. Consider using expressions such as the following:

> We recently heard from our contractor …
> not meet the deadline
> We are sorry … / We regret …
> due to
> some construction noise
> We will do our utmost to …

2. TELEPHONE CONVERSATION: Margaret Smith will respond to Mr. Fuentes' letter by calling him and discussing the situation as she sees it. In her preparation for her telephone call, Ms. Smith will have to decide what her strategy will be and the corresponding tone she will choose to express that strategy (see the written exercises). This will be carried out in pairs, with one member of each team playing the respective roles of Margaret Smith and Raphael Fuentes. The two will not be able to reach agreement over the telephone, and a meeting will be set at Hotel de la Playa. The division of costs for the meeting (air fare, hotel, meals) will be determined over the telephone. After preparing in pairs, some pairs will perform the conversation in front of the class. After each telephone call, the class will evaluate the students' performance on the basis of (1) diplomatic tone [was a tone established which will aid the settling of the disagreement in a mutually satisfying manner], (2) professionality (were the positions presented clearly and firmly without resorting to aggression) and (3) language, both level of sophistication and grammatical correctness. (See Appendix 2: Telephone English)

Ms. Margaret Smith should respond to the telephone conversation with a letter describing what was determined during the telephone conversation with Mr. Fuentes.

3. PRE-NEGOTIATION: Each side will prepare for the negotiations by discussing their negotiation strategy and filling out the Negotiations Worksheet and the Position Presentation Worksheet. (Appendices 3 and 4)

4. MEETING AT THE AIRPORT: Raphael Fuentes will meet the Sun and Fun Tours team at the airport and welcome them. They all know each other from a long business relationship, and so the tone of their conversation will be informal and first names will be used. Naturally, Fuentes will ask about the flight, how business is going, and about the demand for package tours on the British market. He will outline the schedule meetings, dinner, and entertainment for the stay and ask if that is acceptable.

5. THE NEGOTIATIONS: The negotiations should be carried out in a positive tone due to the long business relationship the two teams have enjoyed, the fact that they have a common interest in satisfying the customers, and that they have more to lose than to win by being confrontational.

Teams from Sun and Fun Tours will negotiate with teams from Hotel de la Playa and attempt to reach a satisfactory agreement for both sides. Both teams will have a secretary who records the terms of the agreement as the negotiation proceeds, compares notes upon the completion of the negotiations, and writes up the final agreement.

MEETING AGENDA

1. The demand for a 30 percent reduction to be passed on to the guests
2. Other possible forms of compensation to the guests
3. A guarantee that construction will be limited to the hours between 9 AM to 5 PM
4. The renewing of the contract and its length

6. FINAL AGREEMENT: When a final agreement is reached, it will be summarized to make sure that there are no misunderstandings.

7. PRESENTING AN ANALYSIS OF THE NEGOTIATIONS: Both teams will present the results of their negotiations to the class, as well as their strategy and goals. Finally, the teams will discuss how successful their strategy was in terms of the goals they attained.

LANGUAGE MASTERY EXERCISES

Written Exercises

1. Analyze each sentence and mark it with a letter (A to F) that corresponds to the strategy and tone which best describes it.

___ 1. This delay will cause some problems.

___ 2. I am sure we can work out a mutually satisfying solution.

___ 3. We cannot understand why we were not made aware of this problem earlier.

___ 4. As we see it, there is little we can do about the problem.

___ 5. How do you suggest we solve the problem?

___ 6. We depend on customer satisfaction since much of our business comes from repeat customers.

A. The problem can be solved through mutual effort, and we are willing to cooperate.

B. This is your fault, and we expect you to solve the problem without our help.

C. A statement of fact that indicates that if nothing is done, there will be a problem. This suggests that Sun and Fun Tours expects Hotel de la Playa to propose a solution.

D. Our primary concern is about the welfare of our guests, yet we are not willing to state our position until we hear your position. This suggests that if the Hotel responds positively, that there will be room for negotiations.

E. We are upset with you personally, which is going to place a strain on our relationship.

F. This is basically your fault, but the problem is not insurmountable, which suggests willingness to help solve the problem.

2. The Hotel de la Playa team should write the preliminary letter to Margaret Smith explaining the situation at the hotel and, after their telephone conversation, she should respond in a letter confirming what was discussed.

3. Fill in the Negotiations Worksheet (see Appendix 3) and the Position Presentation Worksheet (see Appendix 4) as part of the pre-negotiation activities.

4. Write up the final agreement. This will be a joint effort completed by the secretaries of both teams.

Oral Exercises

TYING CONCESSIONS TO CONDITIONS

It is not tactically wise to state your concession before making sure that your counterpart is willing to accept the condition on which your concession is contingent. If you introduce your concession first, your counterpart will focus on it rather than on the contingent condition.

In pairs consisting of one representative from Sun and Fun Tours (Student A) and one from Hotel de la Playa (Student B), practice tying concessions to conditions using the following phrases:

On the condition that you …, we could be persuaded to consider the questions of … *(neutral)*

Provided that you …, I think we could consider … *(neutral)*

Provided that you …, we see no objection to … *(more positive)*

If you agreed to …, we could reciprocate with … *(more positive)*

Unless/Only if you …, we would not be prepared to … *(more resistant)*

INITIATING CONCESSIONS TIED TO CONDITIONS (Representative A will make a statement to Representative B.)

Using one of the phrases on the previous page, Student A should suggest a possible concession from Student B as a condition for a possible softening on Student A's demand for a 30 percent reduction. For example, Student A could request compensation if the hours of construction exceed 9 AM to 5 PM as a condition for considering less than a 30 percent price reduction. ("Provided that … we can discuss point 1 and/or 2." This suggests that Student A is willing to accept a compensation less than or other than 30 percent). Then Student A would outline what he or she expects to get on that point (for example, a £20 per day compensation for every day when construction exceeds 9 AM to 5 PM) while trying to withhold as much as possible on what they are willing to give away in terms of the demand of a 30 percent reduction. Naturally, Student B will try to discover as much as possible about what Student A is willing to give away on the question of the 30 percent reduction using statements such as the following:

> However, if we give you £20 per day, are you willing to drop your
> demands for the 30 percent reduction?

Practice the above situations in pairs and then some pairs may be asked to perform their exchange in front of the class.

MAKING DEMANDS TIED TO THE CONCESSIONS MADE

After the first round, where an agreement has been reached, Representative B can make a demand tied to a concession he or she has made. Use the following phrases:

> Student B: We have met one of your major concerns in point 3
> (compensation for construction outside of the hours of
> 9 AM to 5 PM); now let's consider point 4 (length of contract).
>
> We feel that a fair solution would be … (*Here you are not
> making any concession because you suggest in your
> phrasing that you have already made the concession
> in agreeing to point 3.*)

In pairs, practice initiating demands tied to previous concessions, and then some pairs may be asked to present their exchange in front of the class.

COUNTERING A DEMAND WITH A DEMAND OF YOUR OWN

Student B should make a demand. Student A should respond by making a demand with, for example, "Yes, but then we expect you to …"

MODIFYING AN OFFER MADE BY A COUNTERPART

Student A should make an offer. Student B should counter with: "Your offer is acceptable except for one small point …"

Practice modifying an offer in pairs with one representative from each team. Concentrate on issues involved in this case.

ACCEPTING A COMPROMISE

Use the following phrases when accepting a compromise:

> I think that we can accept that.
>
> That appears to be a fair compromise.
>
> I think that we have met half way.

REJECTING A COMPROMISE

> I am afraid that those conditions are unacceptable because ... *(based on the reasons to be stated, but there are still grounds for negotiation)*.
>
> I think we are going to have to reconsider that and get back to you. *(This leaves the opposing team with the choice of a temporary delay in negotiations or modifying their position.)*
>
> I am afraid that we are heading for a deadlock. *(strong)*
>
> I regret that we are dangerously close to having to break off negotiations. *(strong)*

Using *could, would,* and *might*

These three words are useful in tying concessions to conditions. *Could* and *would* are used in hypothetical situations and *might* expresses possibility.

> ***Example:*** If you would meet us half way, say 15 percent, we could accept a 3-year contract.

Complete the following sentences with *could, would* or *might*. (*Might* suggests possibility and is not as definite as *would.*)

1. If you _____ give our guests free meals, we _____ drop our demand for a reduction in price.

2. It _____ be possible to allow the guests access to the swimming pool and tennis courts at a five star hotel.

3. I don't think the guests _____ accept that, but it _____ be worth a try.

4. _____ you accept a 15 percent reduction?

5. It _____ rain tomorrow.

Subject and Verb Agreement

A problem all students have is agreement of subject with verb. The subject and its verb should agree in number and person. All verbs have the same form in the present tense. In the third person singular form, however, add an -s or -es:

	Singular		**Plural**	
First person	I	give/do	we	give/do
Second person	you	give/do	you	give/do
Third person	he/she/it	*gives/does*	they	give/do

Exception: *to be*

	Singular		**Plural**	
First person	I	am	we	are
Second person	you	are	you	are
Third person	he/she/it	is	they	are

Certain words are always singular:

> everyone, everybody, everything
> someone, somebody, something
> no one, nobody, nothing

> ***Example:***
> *Someone* is there.

> information, news, material, money, experience, knowledge, staff, advice, furniture, work, linen

> ***Examples:***
> The *information is* relevant.
> The *linen is* dirty.
> The *news is* good.

There are certain traps to be aware of. For example, study the following sentence:

> *One* of our best customers *is* Sun and Fun Tours.

In this sentence, *one* is the subject of the sentence and not *customers*. *One* is singular and thus we use the verb *is*.

Relative pronouns such as *who, which* and *that* do not determine the verb since they are not the subject of the sentence. In the phrase, "the people who visit us often" *the people* and not *who* is the subject and since *people* is plural the verb must be *visit*, not *visits*.

Complete each sentence with the correct form of the verb in parentheses.

1. The rooms _____ newly remodeled. (to be)

2. The customers who _____ will be given a 20 percent reduction in price. (to complain)

3. The news about the construction schedules _____ not good. (to be)

4. I'm afraid that people _____ not going to be happy with the situation. (to be)

5. I _____ that speaking foreign languages _____ important. (to think, to be)

6. Our guests _____ good service. (to demand)

7. They _____ hard and _____ a good job. (to work, to do)

8. Not everyone _____ to work nights. (to be willing)

The negative form of the simple present is made by the verb *to do* + *not* + the infinitive of the main verb.

> I *don't/do not want* to go out tonight.
> She *doesn't/does not want* to demand too much.

Complete each sentence with the correct negative form of the verb in parentheses.

1. They _____ late at night. (to work)

2. They _____ meals after 10 PM. (to serve)

3. We _____ those terms. (to accept)

4. He _____ likely to agree. (to be)

5. Our president _____ the conditions in the contract. (to like)

Vocabulary Exercise

Use words and phrases from the vocabulary list to complete the sentences.

1. Due to the _____ _____, with lots of rain, Hotel de la Playa claimed _____ _____ and refused to give a discount to Sun and Fun Tours.

2. Sun and Fun Tours _____ a 30 percent _____

    as _____ for the inconvenience caused by the construction
    noise.

3. The _____ ____ _____ between Sun and Fun
    Tours and Hotel de la Playa was equal since they both needed each other.

4. In a win-win approach to _____, both sides have to be

    _____.

5. In order to achieve an _____, both sides have to make

    _____.

VOCABULARY

to achieve, *v.*   To reach your goals

to agree, *v.*   To reach an agreement

agreement, *n.*   Reaching a mutually acceptable compromise

balance of power, *n.*   The power inherent in your position versus
that in the position of the other side

bargaining, *n.* (**to bargain,** *v.*)   Negotiating with the purpose of
coming to an agreement

bargaining power, *n.*   The power of one's position in the negotiation
process

bottom line, *n.*   In this case, the furthest you are willing to go to
reach an agreement. (also: the line at the bottom of a financial report
showing profit or loss)

clientele, *n.*   Customers or clients as a group

compensation, *n.* (**to compensate,** *v.*)   Payment to make good a loss

concession, *n.*   Compromise made by one side in order to reach
an agreement; concessions from one side are expected to be matched by
concessions from the other side

condition, *n.*   The term of a contract or the demand of the bargaining
teams

to confirm, *v.*   To make certain

to convince/persuade, *v.*   To make the other side agree that your
point of view is correct

deadlocked, *adj.*   When negotiations cannot proceed because both
sides are unwilling to compromise

to demand, *v.*   To require/ask for something insistently

demands, *n.*   Your opening position in a negotiation; what you want
your counterpart to accept

discount, *n.*   A reduction from the regular price or value of something

final offer, *n.*   Your last offer before breaking off negotiations

flexibility, *n.*   The state of being flexible

flexible, *adj.*   Willing to negotiate, not rigid in your demands

force majeure, *n.*   A cause or event which neither party has control over such as natural disasters, strikes, or war. Thus, either or both parties may be excused from responsibilities stated in a contract such as delivery dates, dates of completion, and so forth.

half pension, *n.*   In a hotel context it means that guests get breakfast and dinner, but they are on their on for lunch

hardball, softball, *n.*   Describes two approaches to negotiations. The first one suggests inflexibility, where you try to force the opposition to accept your conditions, while the latter suggests a more flexible approach, where you try to reach an acceptable compromise.

to have connections, *v.*   To know people who can help you (business connections)

inclement weather, *n.*   Bad weather

inflexibility, *n.*   The state of being rigid

inflexible, *adj.*   Unwilling to compromise

negotiations, *n.*   The process of bargaining in an attempt to reach a mutually satisfying agreement/contract. to negotiate, v.

objective, *n.*   Your goal; in this case what you hope to obtain

proposal, *n.* **(to propose,** *v.***)**   What you offer as a basis for contract negotiations; **counterproposal,** *n.*   The other side's proposal in response to yours during negotiations

refund, *n.* **(to refund,** *v.***)**   Money paid back to a customer

renegotiations, *n.* **(to renegotiate,** *v.***)**   Negotiations carried out when a contract is renewed

repeat booking, *n.*   Reservation made by the same people year after year

sanction, *n.*   Punishment which can be imposed on the other side if they fail to accept your position

to shy away, *v.*   To avoid

trait, *n.*   A distinguishing quality of personal character; characteristic

strategy, *n.*   The plan you have for achieving your goals

trading card/tradable, *n.*   Demand that you are willing to give up in trade for some of your other demands

ultimatum, *n.*   A final proposal or terms whose rejection will result in the breaking off of negotiations

unyielding, *adj.*   A position of refusing to compromise

SANSUNG SPORTING GOODS SEEKS A SCANDINAVIAN DISTRIBUTOR

An Agency Agreement

CASE SUMMARY

This case involves negotiating an agent agreement between a producer of fishing equipment, Sansung Sporting Goods, and a Scandinavian agent, Scandinavian Sporting Goods Importers.

Distributing products is one of the major aspects of marketing, and although it is possible to open up a sales office in foreign countries, most companies cannot afford the expense. Therefore, many companies choose to use local agents because they can take advantage of the agent's knowledge of consumer habits, advertising approaches, and existing distribution channels. This involves negotiating an agent contract, which is the subject of this case. Negotiating a contract for an ongoing business relationship is a delicate matter. Unlike selling a used car to someone whom you probably will never see again, an agency agreement has to be mutually satisfying if you expect your agent to make a 100 percent effort to sell and distribute your products. Thus, pressuring the agent about 1/4 percent on the commission might be like winning the battle, but losing the war. Naturally, you want to achieve the best possible result for your company, but at the same time you do not want to poison the ongoing business relationship on which your future success depends. Remember that negotiations are a case of give and take, and good negotiators are sensitive to the priorities and musts of the other side. Beating them into submission, even though it may give a sense of victory, is certainly not the way to establish the atmosphere of mutual understanding necessary for an ongoing business relationship.

With this in mind, your preparation must take into consideration both parties' interests. Part of your preparation for the negotiation includes filling out the Negotiations Worksheet in Appendix 3 and the Position Presentation Worksheet in Appendix 4. What follows is a brief summary of how to go about filling out the negotiations worksheet for this case.

I. Goals

In this particular case, you are going to be negotiating (1) rates of commission, (2) an exclusive versus a non-exclusive contract, (3) a fixed price contract versus a flexible price contract, and (4) the covering of advertising, shipping, and storage costs.

You must determine which of these are high priority (musts), medium priority, and low priority. In the latter categories, you have to determine how far you are willing to go in making concessions and what you expect to get in return for your concessions. Some of your low-priority points may be used as trading cards to be given away in their entirety in return for concessions from the other side. However, you should have a clear notion of what you expect to get in return.

II. An Assessment of the Balance of Power

Despite the necessity of a mutually satisfying agreement, both sides will evaluate the strengths and weaknesses of the parties involved in the negotiations in order to avoid being "steamrollered" (dominated by the other side). Assessment of the balance of power will help you to determine your strategy and how much pressure you want to exert on the other party (while not forgetting the importance of a mutually satisfying agreement). Ask yourself some of the basic questions such as how much do we need them, what alternatives do we have, and how viable are those alternatives? Naturally, you must also ask how much they need you.

III. Determining Your Strategy

Your strategy should be a result of your decisions about goals and balance of power. You must determine the bottom line, that is, how far you are willing to go to obtain an agreement. You must also decide what you ideally hope to achieve. The final contract will fall somewhere between these two extremes, and charting them will give you a tool to evaluate the result. There is nothing wrong with shooting for an ideal result as long as your goals do not appear unreasonable, and in meeting resistance, you do not maintain an inflexible position.

Decide on your opening position and the mood you hope to create. As the worksheet shows, there are degrees of positions from hard-line to softer stances. Remember that your opening position will determine the atmosphere for the rest of the negotiations, so choose it with care. Preconditions are usually associated with a hard-line stance; be sure these conditions are an absolute must.

Determine what issues you want to negotiate first. This will help set the tone. If you take the low-priority issues first, you will create a tone of flexibility and good faith. If you are able to create a tone of flexibility on both sides, it will make it easier for you to get what you want on the must items later. Your strategy would be to suggest that you have shown good faith and now it is their turn. On the other hand, starting with the musts will reveal early what the other side's position is on those items most important to you. Since the sensitive negotiator will constantly be listening for clues as to the other side's position and priorities, starting with your musts may give you clues. If you don't meet resistance, go for the maximum. Once you have attained what you want most, you can be flexible on some of the other items in order to create an atmosphere of mutual satisfaction.

To gain insight into your counterpart's position you might "go fishing" to see what bait interests them, which may help you to formulate a clear picture of their strategy. For example, if you are negotiating a contract for a product, you will want to know if price, after-sale service, delivery schedules, warrantees, and so forth are important and in which order. Generally you can talk about these items and see what evokes the most interest.

You should study the subject of negotiation strategy in more detail and discuss your experiences and strategies. However, this outline should give you enough information to solve the case. Fill out the negotiations worksheet, determine your strategy, and be sensitive to possible clues during the negotiations.

The Negotiations Worksheet and the Position Presentation Worksheet, along with a fill-in exercise to help you, are in Appendices 3 and 4.

CULTURAL BACKGROUND

Two groups will be selected by the teacher to present an analysis of the two cultures of negotiations in this case—Korea and Denmark—along the lines discussed in Chapter 2 on cross-cultural negotiations, such as (1) differing concepts of time, (2) the purpose of negotiations—deal versus relationship establishment, (3) approaches to decision making, and (4) the value and importance of protocol, ceremony, and so forth. After each group has presented its culture, both teams will conclude by pointing out areas where, due to differences in the two cultures of negotiation, misunderstanding, frustration, and conflicts might occur.

QUESTIONS FOR DISCUSSION

1. What is the purpose of social activities in negotiations?
2. How important are the social activities in the negotiation culture
    from which you come, and what activities are common in this culture?

CASE

Sansung is a major Korean producer of pleasure boats, which has recently decided to expand into sports fishing equipment, mainly rods and reels. They are a respected company known all over Southeast Asia for quality goods. Their sports fishing equipment has received good reviews, and their prices are competitive with other major brands such as Daiwa, Shakespeare, and Abu.

Their major markets have been Southeast Asia, including Japan, Taiwan, Korea, and Vietnam, countries known for their love of fishing. In their first five years in the field of sports fishing equipment, they have captured the following market shares:

Japan	5%
Taiwan	8%
Korea	15%
Vietnam	7%

The management feels that the company has established itself in these markets and would like to take a step into markets outside of its geographical area. The two potential markets they plan to penetrate are the European and North American. However, they wish to expand cautiously since a failed major expansion could be disastrous. Thus, their strategy is the toe-in-the-water approach, where they pick a small segment of a major market to test their ability to penetrate that market. They have chosen Scandinavia for several reasons.

1. Scandinavians (Norwegians, Swedes, and Danes) are avid outdoors people and sports fishing enthusiasts.
2. They are affluent societies with ample time for outdoor activities and long vacations.
3. They have access to both fresh and salt water fishing.
4. They represent a market of 17 million people, which would be an adequate test market. The Scandinavian market has a considerable profit potential with annual sales for 1996 estimated at:

Denmark	DKK	70 million
Norway		120 million
Sweden		240 million

Studies have shown 40 percent of this market is rods and reels and the remaining 60 percent is terminal tackle (hooks, line, sinkers, etc.)

5. Scandinavians share language and cultural similarities, yet exhibit some cultural differences. This would facilitate producing sales promotion materials, yet provide data on the probable success of the products from three different countries.
6. The Danish-based distributor could further expand distribution into the European Union since Denmark is a member of the EU.

Scandinavian Sporting Goods Importers (SSGI) imports a wide variety of sporting goods equipment in fields such as football, basketball, ice hockey, and skiing and have recently begun importing sports fishing equipment. They do not distribute major brands such as Daiwa and Shakespeare, but have enjoyed success with two minor brands aimed at the popular (low priced) end of the market. They were contacted by Sansung and found the prospect interesting because Sansung produces a complete range of rods and reels at competitive prices, which would allow SSGI to capture greater market shares across the whole range of the market.

For this case, half of the groups will represent Sansung and the other half SSGI. You can have as many negotiations going on at once as you have teams and space.

The basic items in the contract to be decided are the following:

1. *An exclusive contract versus a non-exclusive contract.* In an exclusive contract, Sansung would demand that SSGI distribute only their line of sports fishing equipment, thus dropping the other sports fishing brands that they presently distribute. However, if SSGI accepts this, they could demand exclusive rights to be the sole distributor of Sansung sports fishing equipment in this Scandinavian market.

2. *A fixed price contract versus a flexible price contract.* In a fixed price contract, the price of the goods is fixed once a year. In a flexible price contract, Sansung reserves the right to raise the price of fishing equipment in accordance with a rise in production costs. Naturally, the agent could and probably would pass the rise on to the retailers. However, this would likely cause friction between the distributor and the retailers.

3. *The rate of commission to be paid the distributor, based on the sales price to the retailers in Scandinavia.* You can negotiate a flat commission, for example 25 percent on all sales, or a sliding scale, for example 25 percent on sales up to DKK 10,000,000 and 30 percent on sales from DKK 10,000,000 to DKK 20,000,000, etc.

4. *The covering of advertising costs and approving advertising campaigns.* Who should cover the costs and have the final decision about advertising campaigns?

5. *The covering of shipping expenses* FOB Seoul or CIF (see Vocabulary) and *storage costs* in Denmark. Who should cover these costs?

Negotiate a contract that establishes the conditions for the five points just described.

The Case Sequence

1. PRE-NEGOTIATION: Each side will prepare for the negotiations by discussing their negotiation strategy and filling out the Negotiations Worksheet and the Position Presentation Worksheet. (Appendices 3 and 4)

2. SOCIALIZING: Spend five minutes exchanging business cards and talking about common interests. If you are a fishing enthusiast, share fish stories. If you are golfers, talk about handicaps and the chances of getting in a round of golf. Family is an important item for Koreans and pictures of family are often shown. After-hour socializing is important for Koreans and there might be talk of going to a restaurant.

3. SITTING DOWN AT THE NEGOTIATING TABLE: The Danish host team leader will place the Koreans on the appropriate side of the table with their head of delegation in the middle, surrounded by his subordinates. While still standing, the head of the Danish team will present the team's members, their name and title, and then the head of the Korean team will do the same. Gifts will be exchanged (Koreans are gift givers). In this case, sporting equipment would be appropriate or some business-related items such as pens or desk clocks with the company logo on them, or some items of national art. (See the introduction drill in the exercises for this chapter.)

The Danish Team:

Jens Jespersen, Managing Director
Ole Jensen, Marketing Manager
Kristin Hansen, Sales Manager
Merette Damsgaard, Secretary

The Korean Team:

Chai Lie, Export Manager
Hyung Kim, Marketing Manager
Sam Park, Sales Manager
Suzie Jon, Secretary

4. OPENING STATEMENTS: The head of each team will make a statement of welcome (the Danish) and appreciation for the invitation (the Korean) and their hopes for a mutually satisfying meeting. (See the opening statement suggestions in this chapter.)

5. OPENING THE NEGOTIATIONS: The head of the Danish team will open the negotiations by saying something such as, "Let us proceed then" and suggesting the market potential for Sansung fishing equipment. Naturally, the object is to show that successful negotiations will be profitable for both sides and thus create a positive atmosphere of mutual benefit. The head of the Danish team will then suggest which point the two teams should discuss first by stating, "I suggest we begin with point one, the exclusive contract, if you do not have any objections."

MEETING AGENDA

1. Exclusive versus non-exclusive contract
2. Fixed vs. flexible price contract
3. The rate of commission
4. The covering of advertising costs and who has the final say in approving advertising campaigns
5. The covering of shipping costs

6. CONTINUED NEGOTIATIONS: Negotiations will continue until one or both of the sides feels a need for a break, either to discuss business separately, contact someone at the head office, or simply to get some fresh air. In the latter case, the two teams can socialize outside of the negotiating room, but remember, this is also part of the negotiations process and relevant information can be subtly exchanged. Periodically, throughout the negotiations, particularly when some form of agreement is reached, each team should sum up their understanding of the agreement to avoid misunderstanding. (See the summing up drill in the exercises.)

7. FINAL AGREEMENT: When a final agreement is reached, it will be summarized and then written up in the form of a contract.

8. ANALYSIS OF THE NEGOTIATIONS: Make a presentation where the two teams present the contract arrived at and where each team presents its strategy, its goals, and how successful they were in attaining their goals in the contract.

LANGUAGE MASTERY EXERCISES

Written Exercises

1. Fill in the Negotiations Worksheet (see Appendix 3) and the Position Presentation Worksheet (see Appendix 4) as part of the pre-negotiation activities.
2. Take minutes of the negotiation meeting. Based on these notes, write a report to your respective board of directors along the lines of this chapter's report format.

REPORT

See the report writing format in Appendix 1 and complete the report with the following sections:

      1.0 Pre-Negotiations Strategy
         1.1 Goals
         1.2 Assessment of the balance of power
         1.3 The tone to be established at the beginning of the negotiations
         1.4 The order of discussion of the items (commissions, exclusive contract, etc.)
      2.0 The Negotiations
         2.1 What occurred during the negotiations?
            2.1.1 Did the negotiations follow your strategy, and how successful was your strategy?

3.0 The Tentative Contract Agreement Reached Between Sansung and SSGI

   3.1 Exclusive versus non-exclusive contract

   3.2 Fixed price versus flexible price contract

   3.3 Commission

   3.4 Coverage of advertising costs and authority over advertising campaigns

   3.5 Coverage of shipping expenses

4.0 Recommendation

   4.1 Should your management accept the contract?

   4.2 What impact will this contract have on your company's earnings in the next three years?

Oral Exercises

In pairs, practice the "informal individual introductions" and "seeing people again" exercises. In threes, practice the "introduction of others" exercise. The teacher will select some students to do this in front of the class. The heads of each negotiating team should practice "formal introductions and opening statements" in front of their team and receive feedback about correctness of language and tone. All students should learn the expressions in the "Summing Up" and "Clarifying" sections. They are expected to use them in the negotiations.

INFORMAL INDIVIDUAL INTRODUCTIONS

David Johnson: Hello, David Johnson, Sales Manager."

  Hyung Kim: Hello, Hyung Kim, Marketing Manager, pleased to meet you.

David Johnson: Nice meeting you."   *OR*

                 Pleased to meet you." (with a slight emphasis on the word "you")   *OR*

                 One can simply nod and smile.

Remember that a firm handshake is important. No "dead fish" handshakes, please.

INTRODUCTION OF OTHERS

  David Kim: Mr. Johnson, I would like to introduce you to our marketing manager, Hyung Kim. Hyung, this is David Johnson.

David Johnson: Pleased to meet you, Mr. Kim.

  Hyung Kim: Nice meeting you, Mr. Johnson. (Mr. Kim could also simply say "Nice meeting you.")

SEEING PEOPLE AGAIN

DS: Nice to see you again, Mr. Johnson. How have you been?

RJ: Fine, and you?. How has business been?

Note: Do not use "Nice to meet you again." The verb "to meet" is only used for the first meeting.

FORMAL INTRODUCTIONS AND OPENING STATEMENTS

The head of each delegation is responsible for presenting the members of the team.

Mr. Chai Lie: First, I want to thank you for inviting us here. We look forward to getting to know you better in the course of our stay. I would like to introduce the members of our delegation. My name is Chai Lie and I am Export Manager for Sansung. On my immediate right is Mr. Hyung Kim, our Marketing Manager (Mr. Kim would then make a polite bow). On his right is Mr. Sam Park, our Sales Manager.

Opening statements are geared to expressing welcome or thanks for the invitation and to creating a positive atmosphere. They are characterized by expressions such as:

We would like to welcome you to ...

We are glad that you could come and hope that you will enjoy your stay here. We will do our best to make you feel at home, and if there is anything you need or want, please let us know.

We look forward to getting to know you better both as business partners and socially.

We wish to thank you for inviting us to ... *(formal)*

Thank you for inviting us to ... *(less formal)*

We are looking forward to getting to know you and exploring the opportunities for a profitable business relationship.

(Note the word "exploring," which does not commit the speaker, while "opportunities" and "profitable business relationship" emphasizes the potential and creates a positive tone.)

SUMMING UP

Then we have reached agreement on a commission of 35 percent. (The use of "reached" expresses a common effort and creates a mood of cooperation.)

CLARIFYING

Please correct me if I am wrong, but if I understand you correctly you are proposing ...

Then as I understand it, your offer is ...

I am not sure that I completely understand your offer. Could we go through it again?

Modal Verbs in Polite Requests

In Case 1, we introduced the use of *would* and *could* in hypothetical expressions. They are also used in polite requests. *May* can also be used in polite requests.

> *Could* you help me?
> *Would* you like a cup of coffee?
> *May* I help you?

Since you want to establish good working relations with business associates, for example, an agent, you should know how to use these modal verbs correctly.

Complete the sentences with a correct modal verb.

1. _____ you like to take a break?

2. What _____ you like to drink?

3. _____ I smoke in this room?

4. I _____ like to make a phone call. _____ I use your telephone?

5. I'm going to order a drink. _____ I get you something?

The Simple Present and the Present Continuous

The simple present and the present continuous are the two forms of the present tense. The simple present is the tense used in the subject/verb agreement exercise. It expresses repeated actions, facts, desires, likes, opinions, and ownership.

> I give
> you give
> she gives

> Water *freezes* at 0 degrees centigrade." *(a fact)*
> I *like* to watch basketball. *(likes)*
> He *wants* a new car. *(desires)*
> He *thinks* that there is great market potential in Scandinavia. *(opinion)*
> He *owns* the company. *(ownership)*

Adverbs of frequency such as *every day, always, never, sometimes,* and the like indicate how often something happens, and in the present tense they require the use of the simple present.

> Every day, I get up at six o'clock. *(fact)*

The present continuous expresses something that is happening right now or is temporary. It is formed with the present form of the verb *to be* + the *-ing* form of the main verb.

I am working
you are working
he is working

Words such as *temporarily, for the time being, presently, right now,* and *now* suggest the use of the present continuous.

I *am working* the night shift for the time being. *(temporary)*

He *is serving* dinner right now. *(now)*

The simple present is used much more because we usually talk about actions that are repeated. Think about what you do every day. Most of our actions are repeated again and again. We do not talk about what we are doing right now very often. We use the present continuous as a future tense more than we use it as a present tense.

When *are* you *working* tomorrow?
I'm working the morning shift.

In spoken English, we use the present continuous to express something happening in the future more often than we use the future with *will* (I will…).

Practice the use of the two present tenses. Complete each sentence with the correct form of the verb in parentheses.

1. He _____ to penetrate the Scandinavian market. (to try)

2. They _____ fishing equipment. (to produce)

3. They _____ presently _____ a contract with SSGI. (to negotiate)

4. He _____ a factory in Denmark. (to open)

5. They always _____ a high commission. (to demand)

6. They never _____ for shipping costs. (to pay)

7. They _____ penetrating new markets. (to consider)

8. Why _____ he _____ that there is a good profit potential in Scandinavia? (to think)

Vocabulary Exercise

Complete each sentence with words or phrases from the vocabulary list.

1. We could not agree on the _____ of the contract and thus the negotiations became _____.

2. The most important items in a negotiation are high _____, and the less important items can be used as _____

_____.

3. People who are unyielding are _____.

4. Our _____ _____ was a 25 percent commission. We were not willing to go lower.

5. As importers, we wanted the shipping to be _____, not _____, because it would be cheaper for us.

6. The head of our company, our _____, had good _____ with people in the industry.

7. We could not _____ her to accept our _____.

VOCABULARY

to achieve, *v.*   To reach your goals

to agree, *v.*   to reach an agreement

agreement, *n.*   Reaching a mutually acceptable compromise

balance of power, *n.*   The power inherent in your position versus that in the position of the other side

bargaining, *n.* **(to bargain,** *v.*)   Negotiating with the purpose of coming to an agreement

bargaining power, *n.*   The power of one's position in the negotiation process

bottom line, *n.*   The furthest you are willing to go to reach an agreement (also: the line at the bottom of a financial report showing profit or loss)

CEO, *n.*   Chief Executive Officer, the head of a company

CIF (cost, insurance, freight), *n.*   Where the seller is responsible for all expenses of delivery, including insurance premiums

concessions, *n.*   A compromise made by one side in order to reach an agreement. Concessions from one side are expected to be matched by concessions from the other side.

conditions, *n.*   The terms of a contract or the demands of the bargaining teams

to confirm, *v.*   To make certain

to convince/persuade, *v.*   To make the other side agree that your point of view is correct

deadlocked, *adj.*   When the negotiation process cannot proceed because both sides are unwilling to compromise

demands, *n.*   Your opening position in a negotiation; what you want your counterpart to accept

final offer, *n.*   Your last offer before breaking off of negotiations

flexibility, *n.*   The state of being flexible

flexible, *adj.*   Willing to negotiate, not rigid in your demands

FOB (Free on board), *n.*   Any point to which the transportation costs are borne by the seller and which the title passes to the buyer

to get in on the ground floor, *v.*   To get into a business or market in the beginning so as to take advantage of its growth potential from the beginning

hardball, softball, *n.*   Describes two approaches to negotiations; the first one suggests inflexibility, where you try to force the opposition to accept your conditions, while the latter suggests a more flexible approach, where you try to reach an acceptable compromise

to have connections, *v.*   To know people who can help you (business connections)

inflexibility, *n.*   The state of being rigid

inflexible, *adj.*   Unwilling to compromise

negotiations, *n.* **(to negotiate,** *v.*)   The process of bargaining in an attempt to reach a mutually satisfying agreement/contract

objectives, *n.*   Your goals; what you hope to obtain

priority, *n.*   How you rate something in terms of its importance; high priority, low priority

proposal, *n.* **(to propose,** *v.*)   What you offer as a basis for contract negotiations; **counterproposal,** *n.*   The other side's proposal in response to yours

renegotiations, *n.* **(to renegotiate,** *v.*)   Negotiations carried out when a contract is renewed

sanctions, *n.*   Punishment which can be imposed on the other side if they fail to accept your position

to shy away, *v.*   To avoid

strategy, *n.*   The plan you have to achieve your goals

trading cards/tradables, *n.*   Demands that you are willing to give up in exchange for some of your other demands

traits, *n.*   Characteristics

ultimatum, *n.*   A final proposal or terms whose rejection will result in the breaking off of negotiations

unyielding, *adj.*   A position of refusing to compromise

CASE

3

ACME WATER PUMPS AND THE NIGERIAN GOVERNMENT

A Sales Contract

CASE SUMMARY

One of the major problems in Africa is water supply. One solution is pumping ground water, which saves time and effort for villagers who would otherwise have to walk for miles to sources, some of which are polluted. Another problem is maintenance of technical equipment. African buyers often purchase foreign goods, and they prefer goods that require minimum maintenance. In this case, the Nigerian government is considering buying equipment from an English producer.

The English have had a long tradition of economic and political involvement in Africa. In spite of the colonial nature of past relationships, the English still enjoy a good working relationship with many African governments. Many of the legal, educational, governmental, and value systems which exist today were established by the English and thus there is a common understanding of each other's culture and of how things should be done. However, one major difference is in the rigid government control in Nigeria and the possibility for corruption opened by the centralization of power and lack of democratic controls. This could create conflicts between the English system, which does not condone bribery, and the Nigerian system, which accepts it. Another area of possible conflict is the sense of superior-inferior relationship that may be a by-product of England's relative economic success and Nigeria's economic faltering. Pride will definitely be an issue, and any sense of a superior tone on the part of the English will be counterproductive.

CULTURAL BACKGROUND

Two groups will be selected by the teacher to present an analysis of the two cultures of negotiations in this case—England and Nigeria—along the lines discussed in Chapter 2 on cross-cultural negotiations, such as (1) differing concepts of time, (2) the purpose of negotiations—deal versus relationship establishment, (3) approaches to decision making, and (4) the value and importance of protocol, ceremony, and so forth. Another important issue is tone. What tone should the English delegation establish and what barriers should be overcome? After each group has presented its culture, both teams will conclude by pointing out areas where, due to differences in the two cultures of negotiation, misunderstanding, frustration, and conflicts might occur.

QUESTIONS FOR DISCUSSION

1. Why can negotiations between industrialized and developing countries be particularly sensitive? Why might the two sides be skeptical toward each other?
2. What can be done by both sides to overcome this skepticism?
3. In gauging the balance of power, what advantages does each side have? How would you exploit the advantages of each side? How could each side use their advantages? What is the possible danger of pushing your advantage too far?

CASE

Acme Water Pumps, Ltd. is a major English manufacturer of irrigation equipment whose primary market is Europe, but which is attempting to penetrate the African market. They see a potentially enormous market for their almost maintenance-free J27 water pump. This pump was developed in light of maintenance problems in Africa. The pump is based on a limited number of moving parts, which reduces the need for maintenance and the possibility of breakdowns. They have sent a brochure to the Nigerian Ministry of Agriculture, which has studied the design and shown an interest. The Nigerian Ministry invited the Acme representatives to demonstrate the pump and were openly impressed by both its simplicity and its effectiveness. The ministry extended another invitation to discuss contract matters, which is the basis of this case.

The major items to be negotiated are:

1. *Cost of the pump figured on CIF or FOB.*
    a. *CIF* (Cost, insurance, freight, where the seller is responsible for all of these expenses) or *FOB* (Free on board, where the buyer pays all costs from the moment the goods cross over the ship's rail)
    b. *Delivered at the Frontier*, where the seller's obligations are met when the goods arrive at the frontier/border or *Delivered Duty Paid*, where the seller must deliver to the buyer's door and pay all of the duties.

2. *Credit terms.* A common credit term is 30 days, 1 percent, which means that the Nigerians will receive a 1 percent discount if they pay within 30 days of the billing date. With this system, however, there is no guarantee that they will pay. For that, the British would need an irrevocable documentary credit. (See Vocabulary)

3. *Installation of the pumps.* Installation of the pumps will involve an expense for Acme. Naturally, the more pumps ordered, the lower the installation fee per pump. At a certain level of purchase, the installation should be free.

4. *A service contract and the training of Nigerian nationals to man the service center.* The Nigerians are interested in a service center being established which would eventually be manned by Nigerians. This would result in jobs and training and reduce service costs.

5. *The possibility of a subsidiary jointly owned by Acme and a Nigerian partner.* The Nigerians would want a joint venture that would result in jobs, training, technology transfer, and profits.

The Case Sequence

1. PRE-NEGOTIATION: Each side will prepare for the negotiations by discussing their negotiation strategy and filling out the Negotiations Worksheet and the Position Presentation Worksheet. (Appendices 3 and 4)

2. SOCIALIZING: Spend five minutes exchanging business cards and talking about common interests.

3. SITTING DOWN AT THE NEGOTIATING TABLE: The Nigerian team leader, Mr. John Abiola, Deputy Secretary for the Ministry of Agriculture, will place the English on the appropriate side of the table with their head of delegation in the middle, surrounded by his subordinates. While still standing, the head of the Nigerian team will introduce the team's members, their name and title. Then the head of the English team, David Smythe, Head of Overseas Sales will do the same. (See "Formal Introduction and Opening Statements" in Case 2.)

The Nigerian Team:

Mr. Christian Onoh, Chief Engineer for Irrigation Projects
Mr. Stephen Agu, Chief Purchaser
Mr. Jim Nwododo, Agricultural Consultant
Mr. Paul Nwankwo, Comptroller

The English Team:

Mr. Richard Bromhead, Product Manager for the J27 water pump
Mr. Ian Barnard, Area Representative for Africa
Mr. Robert Cooper, Head of Production
Mr. George Wallace, Head of Service and Installation

4. OPENING STATEMENTS: The head of each team will make a statement. John Abiola will welcome the English team and then David Smythe will thank the Nigerian head for the invitation. Both will express a desire for a lasting mutually beneficial relationship and emphasize the enormous agricultural potential to be developed in Nigeria through irrigation projects. This also means that the Nigerian villages would enjoy the advantages of having easy access to water.

5. OPENING THE NEGOTIATIONS: The head of the Nigerian team will suggest which item to begin with stating: "I suggest that we begin with …"

MEETING AGENDA

1. Cost of pumps
2. Coverage of shipping costs (CIF or FOB)
3. Credit terms
4. Installation of pumps
5. The service contract
6. A jointly owned subsidiary

6. CONTINUED NEGOTIATIONS: Negotiations will continue until one or both of the sides feel a need for a break, either to discuss business separately, contact someone at the Ministry, or simply to get some fresh air. In the latter case the two teams can socialize outside of the negotiating room, but remember, this is also part of the negotiation process and relevant information can be subtly exchanged. Periodically throughout the negotiations, particularly when some form of agreement is reached, each team should sum up their understanding of the agreement to avoid misunderstanding.

7. FINAL AGREEMENT: If a final agreement is reached, it will be summarized and then written up in the form of a contract.

8. ANALYSIS OF THE NEGOTIATIONS: Make a presentation where the two teams present the contract arrived at and where each team presents its strategy, its goals, and how successful the team members feel they were in attaining their goals in the contract.

LANGUAGE MASTERY EXERCISES

Written Exercises

1. Fill in the Negotiations Worksheet (see Appendix 3) and the Position Presentation Worksheet (see Appendix 4) as part of the pre-negotiation activities.

2. If you arrive at an agreement, write up a final contract as a joint assignment involving both teams.

Oral Exercises

Review the oral exercises (formal introductions, opening statements, summing up, and clarifying) in Case 2, "Sansung Sporting Goods Seeks a Scandinavian Distributor" and be prepared to use them in this case.

Using Qualifiers

To avoid being blunt it is wise to use qualifiers such as *might, could possibly, a slight, quite, could* and *would.*

Instead of saying "That is impossible" it is more diplomatic to say "That might be difficult." Diplomatic expressions are extremely important in negotiations since they allow you to create a diplomatic tone. It is also important that you avoid using words that have a negative prefix (*im-, un-, il-*) such as *impossible, unnecessary,* and *illogical.* Instead, use a positive expression with a qualifier. "This is impossible" sounds more diplomatic if you said, "This might not be possible. When rejecting a proposal, you can often use the expression "I'm afraid that ...."

Change the following sentences to make them sound more diplomatic.

1. Your proposal is unacceptable.
2. Your statistics are wrong.
3. That will create a problem.
4. We can't do that.
5. That's impossible.

Past Tense

The two past tenses which you will use the most are the simple past and the present perfect. The simple past expresses an action completed at a definite time in the past.

I *ate* dinner at 7 o'clock last night.

The present perfect consists of the present form of the verb *to have* and the *past participle* of the main verb.

I have	we have	
you have	you have	+ the past participle of the main verb
he/she has	they have	

I *have worked* here for four years.

The present perfect expresses two types of action.

a. An action that begun in the past and is continuing up to the present.

We have developed our infrastructure over the past ten years.

This sentence tells you that the people are still developing the infrastructure (a continuing process over the last ten years).

b. An action that occurred at an indefinite time in the past.

We have built a power plant.

This sentence tells you that the power plant was completed, but it does not tell when.

Practice the use of the two past tenses by completing each sentence with the correct form of the verb in parentheses.

1. We _____ the possibilities of developing a resort in your country. (to look into)

2. Our analysis of the market potential, _____ last year,

    _____ very positive. (to make, to be)

3. For six years, we _____ the question of tourism in our country. (to debate)

4. Last year, we _____ a similar proposal. (to reject)

5. Yesterday, you _____ that, three years ago, you

    _____ similar programs in other African countries.
    (to say, to develop)

6. We _____ several projects and they

    _____ very beneficial for the European developers,

    but not for the host country. (to see, to be)

Vocabulary Exercise

Complete each sentence with words and phrases from the vocabulary.

1. For an importer, shipping costs paid _____ are cheaper

    than paid _____.

2. _____ means to fail to pay one's debts. If Acme is afraid of

   this, they will ask for _____ _____

   _____.

3. Acme wants to use Nigeria _____ _____ the East African market.

4. The Nigerians want Acme to hire Nigerian _____ and to

   open a _____.

5. If the Nigerians purchase a large number of pumps, they will probably

   get a _____.

VOCABULARY

CIF (cost, insurance, freight), *adj.* Where the seller is responsible for all expenses of delivery, including insurance premiums

clerical staff, *n.* The personnel dealing with office work such as filing, typing, and billing

to default, *n.* To fail to pay your debts

delivered at the frontier Delivery where the seller's obligations are met when the goods arrive at the frontier/border. The buyer must get the goods through.customs and arrange to get them delivered to their door

delivery duty paid Delivery where the seller must deliver to the buyer's door and pay all of the duties

discount, *n.* **(to discount,** *v.)* A reduction in price

FOB (Free on board), *adj.* Free on board, where the buyer pays all costs from the moment the goods cross over the ship's rail

irrevocable documentary credit, *n.* A means of payment where money is placed with a third party, a bank, and is transferred to the seller upon delivery of the goods. Irrevocable means that this arrangement cannot be changed or canceled.

nationals, *n.* Citizens of the country in question (in this case, Nigerians)

to penetrate, *n.* In this case to enter a new market

subsidiary, *n.* A company in which more than half of the share capital is owned by another company

AMERICAN AUTO CORP.
VS. THE MEXICAN
AUTO WORKERS' UNION

Wage
and Working Conditions
Negotiations

CASE SUMMARY

Due to the low cost and high skill of Mexican labor, as well as NAFTA (see Vocabulary) many American companies have established factories in Mexico. Running factories involves negotiating wages and working conditions, which is the focus of this case.

Labor contract negotiations are unique in that both parties approach the negotiations from opposite directions. Whereas management is used to top-down decision making, labor union representatives must answer to their members, and thus their decision-making process is bottom-up. When management arrives at a decision, the decision is final, but the union representatives must submit the contract to its members for approval. Thus, the union representatives enjoy less freedom of movement during negotiations, a fact which is often overlooked by management. Management can view the union representatives as being inflexible when they are simply aware of how far they can go and still get the contract accepted by the union members.

In addition, this case between Mexican workers and American management introduces other possible sources of conflict. Americans, los gringos, can easily be perceived as the exploiters who are trying to take advantage of low Mexican wages, lax environmental laws, and weaker unions. In addition, the Americans can easily be perceived as rich enough to meet union demands. The fact that the American executives also have their budgets is often overlooked.

CULTURAL BACKGROUND

Your teacher will select two groups to present an analysis of the two cultures of negotiations in this case—Mexico and the United States—along the lines discussed in Chapter 2 on cross-cultural negotiations, such as (1) differing concepts of time, (2) the purpose of negotiations—deal versus relationship establishment, (3) confrontation and emotion in negotiating and (4) the value and importance of protocol, ceremony, and so forth. In addition, the discussion should include possible conflicts arising from perceptions of each other resulting from events in Mexican-American history. Include in this the recent initiation of NAFTA (The North American Free Trade Agreement) and how it is perceived by both sides. After each group has presented its culture, both teams will conclude by pointing out areas where, due to differences in the two cultures of negotiation, misunderstanding, frustration, and conflicts might occur.

QUESTIONS FOR DISCUSSION

1. What disadvantages do national unions face when dealing with multinational companies?
2. What advantages would the Mexican union have in arguing their case with American Auto Corp.?
3. How would a management team from your country approach negotiations with the Mexican union? What would their attitude be, cooperative or combative? On what points would they be flexible and on what points would they be resistant?

CASE

The annual wage and working conditions negotiations are imminent, and both management for American Auto Corp. de Mexico and the union representatives have started preparing for them. American and Japanese auto producers have poured billions of dollars into the Mexican auto industry due to low wages, increasing productivity, and increased access to North American markets as a result of NAFTA. An upswing in the Mexican economy has also increased optimism concerning the Mexican automotive industry's future. Domestic vehicle sales are expected to grow at a 10 percent annual rate over the next four years. Productivity figures are very impressive, increasing 12.5 percent in the previous year compared to 6.3 percent the year before. Similar figures for the previous year in the United States were only 3 percent. A comparison of the average value of the costs per unit indicates that Mexico was 6 percent lower than the United States. Rationalization of the Mexican factories is expected to create an even greater gap between production costs per unit in Mexico and the United States in the coming years. In addition, Mexican plants have received a number of international quality awards reflecting the dedication of Mexican workers to quality. Mexican plants have shown their ability to respond quickly to new market demands by adapting production lines accordingly. Thus, they are expected to play a major role in North American auto production, both for American and other major automobile producers. However, Mexican workers still lag far behind their American counterparts making only $2.50 per hour versus $12.00 per hour. Further grievances are the working conditions. In spite of the installation of state-of-the-art production equipment in the Hermosillo plant, American Auto Corp. did not invest in adequate air-conditioning, ventilation, and soundproofing equipment. Thus, working conditions can be described as a living hell, due to 40 degree centigrade temperatures, poor air quality, and sound levels of 120 decibels (90 decibels being considered an absolute maximum level). Not only is the plant polluted, but the area around it has suffered due to increased pollution. Smog now hangs over Hermosillo, and increased levels of respiratory diseases and nausea are the result. In addition, there are signs that the ground water, which supplies much of the local drinking water, is polluted, allegedly from the factory waste, which is not treated before being dumped into the local river.

From management's side, the two basic complaints are high absenteeism (20 percent above a comparable U. S. plant) and higher-than-expected cost per unit levels. Granted that cost per unit is lower than in the United States, but given the labor costs, management expected an even lower cost per unit rate. Still, Mexico plays an important role in American automobile producers' global strategy, not only because of lower production costs and increasing quality, but also due to the availability of raw materials such as copper, steel, and lead and a wide variety of plastics, which are a by-product of Mexico's oil industry. Recent foreign investments of $3 billion reflect Mexico's place in the automobile industry's game plan.

Both union and management have had a long-term relationship, and in preliminary discussions the Automobile Workers Union of Mexico has made the following demands. The management team must prepare for the negotiations on the basis of these demands and the union team on the basis of the expected management response to these demands. (The union team will write out an agenda for the meeting based on these demands.)

Responding to a questionnaire, the union has decided to demand the following:

NON-REMUNERATIVE DEMANDS

1. A no-layoff guarantee
2. Installation of an air-conditioning system to maintain a maximum temperature of 30 degrees centigrade. Estimated cost $10 million.
3. Installation of a ventilation system to remove up to 85 percent of all dust and other particles from the air in the factory. Estimated cost $7 million.
4. Soundproofing to reduce the maximum decibel level to 75. Estimated cost $6 million.
5. Installation of cleansing systems on the factory's smoke stacks to remove 95 percent of all pollutants emanating from them. Estimated cost $5 million.
6. Financing the connection of the factory to the city's waste treatment center and the extra municipal expenditure to upgrade the facility to handle the additional waste. Estimated cost $10 million.

REMUNERATION DEMANDS

1. A 20 percent across-the-board raise
2. Twenty days a year sick leave with pay (At present workers have 10 days.)
3. COLA (Cost of living adjustment) compensation for inflation so that wage increases represent real wage increases

The Case Sequence

1. PRE-NEGOTIATION: Each side will prepare for the negotiations by discussing their negotiation strategy and filling out the Negotiations Worksheet and the Position Presentation Worksheet. (Appendices 3 and 4)

2. SOCIALIZING: Spend five minutes talking about common interests including the situation at the factory. You know each other well, but the tone may be a bit formal since the union team is particularly skeptical about what position the management team will take. The management team can set the mood by the tone they establish.

3. SITTING DOWN AT THE NEGOTIATING TABLE: Without much formality the two teams will seat themselves at the negotiating table.

4. OPENING STATEMENTS: The opening statements will be important because they will set the tone for the remainder of the negotiations. Choose them strategically.

5. OPENING THE NEGOTIATIONS: The head of the management team will open the negotiations with a statement such as, "Let's get down to business. I suggest that we begin with item ... on the agenda." Then the head of the union team will either agree or suggest another item. Once there is agreement on the item, the negotiations can proceed. The same procedure will be followed for each new item to be discussed.

6. CONTINUED NEGOTIATIONS: Negotiations will continue until one or both of the sides feels a need for a break, either to discuss business separately, contact someone at the head office, or simply to get some fresh air. In the latter case, the two teams can socialize outside of the negotiating room, but remember, this is also part of the negotiation process and relevant information can be subtly exchanged. Periodically, throughout the negotiations, particularly when some form of agreement is reached, each team should sum up their understanding of the agreement to avoid misunderstanding.

7. FINAL AGREEMENT: When a final agreement is reached, it will be summarized to ensure that there is no misunderstanding.

8. ANALYSIS OF THE NEGOTIATIONS: Make a presentation in which the two teams present the contract arrived at and each team presents its strategy, its goals, and how successful they were in attaining their goals in the contract.

LANGUAGE MASTERY EXERCISES

Written Exercises

1. Fill in the Negotiations Worksheet (see Appendix 3) and the Position Presentation Worksheet (see Appendix 4) as part of the pre-negotiation activities.
2. Take minutes of the negotiation meeting. Based on these notes, management will write a report to its board of directors and the union representatives to its members along the lines of the report format in Appendix 1.

Oral Exercises

In pairs, practice the Polite, Diplomatic, and Strategic Language exercises in Appendix 5.

Double Negatives

This case involves a Spanish-speaking team. A typical problem for Spanish speakers is double negatives. In Spanish, it is correct to say, "No tengo nada," which translates, "I don't have nothing" with two negatives. In English, the correct way to say this is, "I don't have anything" or "I have nothing." This also raises the question of the use of *nothing, no one,* and *nobody* or *something, someone,* and *somebody.* We use *someone, something,* and *somebody* in affirmative statements.

I would like *someone* to help me.

Anyone, anything, and *anybody* are used in negative statements and in questions.

I don't have *anything.*
Do you have *anything* that I can use?

One exception to this rule is asking polite questions. For example, the question, "Would you like any coffee?" might sound as if you expect the person to say, "no." Thus, the most polite question would be, "Would you like some coffee?"

Complete these statements and questions with *any, some, anything, anyone, anybody, something, someone, nothing, no one,* and *nobody.*

1. I don't want _____ coffee.

2. Would you like _____ tea?

3. I'm sorry, but we don't have _____ more. We are sold out.

4. There is _____ I want to talk to you about.

5. Is there _____ you want to add to what I have just said?

6. There is _____ whom I know who can help us.

7. Why hasn't _____ been done?

Vocabulary Exercise

Use words and phrases from the vocabulary list to complete the sentences.

1. The union demanded a 10 percent _____-_____-

    _____ wage increase so that everyone would have the

    same percentage raise.

2. The union also demanded _____ as a compensation
    for inflation.

3. They did not accept the management's proposal of 5 percent and made a

    _____ of 7.5 percent.

4. If management didn't meet their demands, the union threatened a

    _____. Management made a counterthreat of a

    _____.

5. It looks as if the negotiations were _____ since the two

    sides could not reach an _____. So they suggested

    — _____, submitting the decision to a third party.

VOCABULARY

across-the-board increase, *n.*   A wage increase given to all or nearly all employees at one time. This is in the form of a percentage or dollar and cents increase, say 5 percent or $0.50 per hour.

agreement, *n.*   A contract or mutual understanding between a union and a company, setting forth the terms and conditions of employment such as salaries, benefits, and other working conditions

apprentice, *n.*   One who is learning a trade or craft and who receives lower wages than a journeyman

arbitration, *n.* Parties unable to agree on a contract submit the final decision to a third party; **an arbitrator,** *n.*

bargaining, *n.* Negotiating a contract—in this case, a contract to set forth the conditions of employment

bottom line, *n.* In this case, as far as you are willing to go to meet the other party to reach an agreement

COLAs (Cost of Living Adjustments), *n.* Compensation for inflation so that wage increases represent real wage increases. This is a common union demand, but at present, COLAs are rarely awarded by management.

collective bargaining, *n.* The process where representatives from the union and management work out a contract specifying the conditions of employment.

counterproposal, *n.* An offer made in response to an offer made by the other party in negotiations

deadlocked, *adj.* When negotiations reach an impasse and no further progress can be made. In this case, the decision can be turned over to an arbitrator.

downsizing, *n.* Reducing the size of a company's workforce.

earnings, *n.* The amount of money received by a worker, including salary, bonuses, commissions, overtime pay, etc.

to employ, *v.* To hire

employee, *n.* Anyone who works for an employer

employer, *n.* A person, association, or company having workers in its employ

grievance, *n.* Any complaint by an employee or by a union about any aspect of employment

journeyman, *n.* A worker in a craft or trade who has served an apprenticeship and is qualified for employment at the journeyman's rate of pay

layoff, *n.* Temporary or indefinite termination of employment, usually due to a lack of work. This is not the same as discharge (firing).

lockout, *n.* When unions refuse to accept an employer's conditions, the employer can close the factory to the present employees and even hire new employees. This is the employer's sanction which corresponds to the union's sanction of a strike.

market share, *n.* The percentage of the total market that a product has

mediation, *n.* A situation in which a neutral person **(a mediator)** works with labor and management to help them reach an agreement

musts, *n.* Important demands that you must get if you are going to accept an agreement

NAFTA, *n.*   The North American Free Trade Agreement is an agreement to lower tariffs between Canada, The United States, and Mexico to facilitate the free flow of goods, and services

natural attrition (British: **natural wastage**) *n.*   Reducing the workforce through retirement and not layoffs

negotiations, *n.* Discussion with the intent of reaching an agreement

picket, *n.*   One who does the picketing

picketing, *n.*   The act of patrolling at or near the employer's place of business during a strike to inform the public that there is a labor dispute in progress or to prevent strikebreakers from entering the place of employment.

productivity, *n.*   An index to measure the efficiency of a plant in utilizing its manpower and equipment

raise (British: **rise**), *n.*   An increase in wages

ratification, *n.*   The acceptance by the members of a union of a contract worked out between the representatives of the union and management

real wages, *n.*   The real worth of one's wages (present and future) in terms of buying power; this is affected by inflation

recession, *n.*   A temporary decline in business activity

seniority, *n.*   The length of time an employee has worked at a company; this frequently determines the priority where promotions and layoffs are concerned

shift, *n.*   The set period of time one works, for example 8 AM-4 PM

shift differential, *n.*   Different rates of pay for different shifts

shop steward, *n.*   The representative of the union at the place of work

strike, *n.*   A work stoppage on the part of the employees to force management to meet union's demands

strikebreaker, *n.*   Employees hired while the original workforce is on strike so that the company can continue its operations; also called **scabs** (a derogatory expression)

strike fund, *n.*   The amount of money a union has to support its workers while they are on strike

trading cards, *n.*   Demands that you are willing to give away to get the most important demands—your musts—during negotiations

wage, *n.*   The price paid by the employer for work or services rendered by an employee

wage cut, *n.*   A reduction in wages

workday, *n.*   The time spent by an employee at work during a normal day, usually eight hours

HYDRA TECH
AND BERTONI SHIPPING

Product Presentation
and a Sales Contract

CASE SUMMARY

This case involves both selling a product and negotiating a sales contract between a German producer of hydraulic cranes and an Italian shipping company. Remember, in such cases, a major part of negotiating is convincing the other party that they need your product. Germany has an excellent reputation for producing quality goods, and German salespeople often emphasize the technological quality of their products when selling. However, there is a modern trend in sales that emphasizes a customer orientation, which means that a salesperson should focus on the customer's needs and show how his or her product meets these needs. Thus, a product-oriented salesperson misses the point in presenting only the technological advantages of the product, while forgetting that the product must perform in a given situation to meet the customer's needs. An understanding of these needs, and a tailoring of the sales presentation to show how the product satisfies these needs, is important. In this case, there are considerations such as delivery, service, training, and credit terms. Your job as salesperson is to analyze your customer's needs and show how the total package best meets these needs. To help you make a good presentation, see the "Making a Good Presentation" section in Case 10.

CULTURAL BACKGROUND

Perhaps one major difference between the German and Italian considerations would be an emphasis on the technological qualities of the product from the German side and the Italian shipping company's concern with delivery schedules, training, service, and credit terms. The German culture prizes technological advancement and emphasizes this in sales promotion. Naturally, the quality of the machines is important; however, Bertoni's concerns go beyond pure quality concerns. Two groups will be selected by the teacher to present an analysis of the two cultures of negotiations in this case—Germany and Italy—along the lines discussed in Chapter 2 on cross-cultural negotiations, such as (1) differing concepts of time, (2) the purpose of negotiations—deal versus relationship establishment, (3) approaches to decision making, and (4) the value and importance of protocol, ceremony, and so forth. After each group has presented its culture, both teams will conclude by pointing out areas where, due to differences in the two cultures of negotiation, misunderstanding, frustration, and conflicts might occur.

QUESTIONS FOR DISCUSSION

1. When selling a product in your culture, what is of greater importance—a product orientation where you emphasize the quality of the product or a customer orientation where you emphasize how the product will benefit the customer and meet his or her needs?

2. How would you present Hydra Tech's product? Each group will discuss this and then several groups will be asked to make a brief presentation of Hydra Tech's cranes to a Bertoni representative. Afterward, the class will evaluate the presentations on the basis of how convincing they were and the language they used.

CASE

Hydra Tech, GmbH is a major producer of hydraulic cranes for both maritime and construction purposes. They are recognized for the quality of their cranes and the inventiveness of their design. The company has produced a low-profile crane with low height, weight, and center of gravity, which allow it to operate in narrow conditions and to pass under low bridges. They have a worldwide service network available 24 hours a day. Mounting of cranes can be done by Hydra Tech's service personnel or by the customer, who is supplied with simple installation manuals. Bertoni Shipping, which operates out of Genoa, is a new but rapidly expanding shipping company specializing in bulk cargo. Bertoni's major concerns are the quality of the product, and thus providing reduced chances of breakdown, speed of loading, worldwide service facilities, training, delivery, and mounting of cranes. They are an interesting customer due to their rapid expansion and good cash flow, which makes them a good credit risk. Hydra Tech would consider winning the first contract an important step in getting in on the ground floor of an expanding company.

Bertoni's engineers have seen Hydra Tech's All Purpose Service Crane, which has twice the capacity of their present cranes. They were interested in a crane with a 25-ton lift capacity whose book price was DM 590,000, with a one year all parts and labor warranty. The cost of mounting the cranes was quoted at DM 7,000 at Genoa. Following a discussion with the engineers, the Chief Purchaser, Roberto Marchelli, contacted Dieter Schmidt, the Head of European Sales for Hydra Tech, to discuss details of a contract for an initial purchase of ten cranes of the type described.

Items to be negotiated are:

1. *Price of the cranes.* The crane's list price is DM 590,000, but no doubt a discount could be arranged based on the quantity of purchase.

2. *Price of mounting.* The standard price is DM 7,000 per unit, but a discount could be arranged if there were a number of cranes to be mounted at one time.

3. *The length of the warranty.* The normal warranty is one year.

4. *Lag time between order and delivery, and penalty for late delivery.* Normal lag time is three months, which Hydra Tech rarely has any trouble meeting. However, Hydra Tech has never had late delivery penalties in their contracts.

5. *Credit terms.* Common credit terms are 30 days, 1 percent. (See Vocabulary)

6. *Training in the operation of the cranes.* Free training is not uncommon.

The Case Sequence

1. PRE-NEGOTIATIONS: Roberto Marchelli will contact Dieter Schmidt by phone to arrange a meeting in Genoa. He will express his interest in the cranes and set a time for the meeting. This is to be done in pairs, with one person playing Marchelli and one playing Schmidt. After preparing in pairs, some pairs will perform the conversation in front of the class. After each telephone call, the class will evaluate the students' performance on the basis of language, including both level of sophistication and grammatical correctness. (See Appendix 2: Telephone English)

Each side will prepare for the negotiations by discussing their negotiation strategy and filling out the Negotiations Worksheet and the Position Presentation Worksheet. (See Appendices 3 and 4)

2. SOCIALIZING: You will get to know the members of the other team. The tone will be formal, and each team member will introduce himself or herself.

3. SITTING DOWN AT THE NEGOTIATING TABLE: Marchelli will show the German team to the negotiating table. Each head of team, starting with Bertoni Shipping, will introduce the team members, their name, and title.

The Bertoni Team:
Roberto Marchelli, Chief Purchaser
Antonio Bagio, Comptroller
Victoria Antonelli, Corporate Counsel
Marco David, Chief Engineer

The Hydra Tech Team:
Dieter Schmidt, Head of European Sales
Gustav Kneidl, Chief Engineer
Thomas Weil, Production Manager
Heidi Stein, Installation and Service Manager

4. OPENING STATEMENTS: Marchelli will make a brief statement of welcome. Dieter Schmidt will thank him for the invitation.

5. OPENING THE NEGOTIATIONS: Marchelli will open the negotiation by saying something such as, "I suggest we begin with ..." and suggest the first point to be discussed.

MEETING AGENDA

1. Price of the cranes
2. Price of mounting
3. The length of the warranty
4. Lag time between order and delivery, and penalty for late delivery
5. Credit terms
6. Training in operation of the cranes

6. CONTINUED NEGOTIATIONS: Negotiations will continue until one or both of the sides feels a need for a break, either to discuss business separately, contact someone at the head office, or simply to get some fresh air. In the latter case, the two teams can socialize outside of the negotiating room, but remember, this is also part of the negotiation process and relevant information can be subtly exchanged. Periodically, throughout the negotiations, particularly when some form of agreement is reached, each team should sum up their understanding of the agreement to avoid misunderstanding.

7. FINAL AGREEMENT: When a final agreement is reached, it will be summarized and then written up in the form of a contract.

8. ANALYSIS OF THE NEGOTIATIONS: Make a presentation in which the two teams present the contract arrived at and each team presents its strategy, its goals, and how successful they were in attaining their goals in the contract.

LANGUAGE MASTERY EXERCISES

Written Exercises

1. Fill in the Negotiations Worksheet (see Appendix 3) and the Position Presentation Worksheet (see Appendix 4) as part of the pre-negotiation activities.
2. If you arrive at an agreement, write up a final contract as a joint assignment involving both teams.

Oral Exercise

Respond to the following statements. Practice them in pairs, and then present the dialogue in front of the class for evaluation on both correctness of language and skillfulness of tactics.

Bertoni Representative (BR)	Hydra Tech Representative (HTR)
1. "Good morning. Thank you for coming to Genoa."	"My pleasure. I hope that you found our offer interesting."
2. "Yes, but …" (Express that there are certain things which must be discussed.)	Ask which ones.
3. "I would like to discuss your price. DM 590,000 seems high, especially when we are buying 10 cranes."	"However, …" (Emphasize the quality of your cranes and the money to be saved in using them.)
4. "Yes, but …" (Emphasize the fact that you are purchasing ten cranes now and possibly many more later.)	Respond to this argument.
5. If the response in number 4 is satisfactory, move on to point 6. If you are dissatisfied, express your disappointment and say that you have better offers.	Respond to BR. Consider making a concession by adding something free or question whether the other cranes can perform as well as yours.
5a. Respond to HTR's question/ concession.	
6. "There are some other problems with your offer."	Find out what the problems are.
7. Explain the first problem and make a demand. Begin with the warranty only being for one year.	Respond, saying that this is standard in the industry. Emphasize the quality of your cranes.
8. Respond to HTR's statement and discuss back and forth until this issue is solved.	
9. Take up the question of credit terms and ask for 30 days, 1 percent.	Respond by stating that your normal terms are 30 days with no discount.
10. Interpret this statement and respond strategically.	Respond to BR's response.

Phrases to be used in the oral exercise:

> There are a couple of points we must discuss.
>
> I hope that we can settle a few points.
>
> When purchasing so many units, one would expect a discount.
>
> How would you feel if we were to include ... free of cost?
>
> If you accept ... we could consider ...
>
> I'm afraid we have a much better offer.
>
> Remember price is not everything. We can offer you ..., which the others cannot.
>
> Our offer is both technically and service-wise the best in the industry.
>
> Being a potential key customer, we would expect ... / We had hoped that you could offer ... / Think of your offer in terms of our total potential purchase.
>
> Yes, I think we can agree to that.
>
> I'm afraid that I do not have the authority to make that decision. I will have to check with headquarters and get back to you.

There is/are and *It is*

In giving directions and information you often use *there is/are* or *it is*. However, you must know which one to use and when.

1. *There is/are*

When you are giving new information or point at something concrete, you use *there is/are*.

> *There is* a bus parked in front of the hotel.
> *There are* telephone boxes over there.
> *There are* three vacant rooms.

The choice of *is* or *are* is determined by the object (a bus/rooms). If the object is singular (a bus) then use *is*. If the object is plural (rooms), then use *are*.

2. *It is*

The three standard uses of *it is* are:

> a. Time: *It is* three o'clock.
> b. Weather: *It is* a nice day. It is rainy/foggy/sunny/cloudy/hot/humid/dry.
> c. *It is* + an adjective: *It is* easy/difficult/clean/dirty.

When you have an *adjective + a noun*, then it is the noun that determines the correct form.

> *It is* hard. (adjective and no noun)
> *There are* hard times ahead. (The plural noun "times" determines that you must use *there are*.)

Complete these sentences with either *there is/there are,* or *it is.*

1. _____ easy to understand why they are the leader in the industry.

2. _____ many models on the market, but none as good as Hydra Tech's.

3. _____ the newest model on the market.

4. _____ only 15 cranes in stock.

5. _____ difficult to predict the market for cranes in the future.

6. _____ one model that I would recommend to you.

7. _____ a possibility that we could get a discount?

8. _____ any questions?

9. _____ difficult times ahead.

10. _____ a call for you on line one.

Introduction and Follow Up

You introduce new information or point out a physical object with *there is/are.*
However, when you continue to talk about it, you use *it is/they are.*

> *There is* a book on the table. *It is* red.

> *There are* two telephone directories on the table. *They are* for Oslo
> and Stockholm.

This rule holds true no matter what tense you are using.

Introduction	*Follow up*
There is	It is
There are	They are
There was	It was
There were	They were
There will be a conference	It will be
There will be two conferences	They will be

Complete the following sentences, using *there is, there are, it is, there was, there were, it was, they were, there will be, it will be,* or *they will be.*

1. _____ a conference on the subject of cancer research in June. _____ in Stockholm. _____ 500 delegates. _____ from all over the world.

2. _____ a new computerized reservation system on the market. _____ very efficient. _____ an instruction manual which comes with it. _____ easy to understand. _____ a course to teach us how to use the system. _____ next week.

3. _____ a meeting yesterday. _____ about initiating a new computer system. _____ representatives from the staff and management. _____ a lot of discussion, but no decision was made.

Vocabulary Exercise

Complete the sentences with words and phrases from the vocabulary list.

1. The company had poor _____ _____ and had to borrow money.

2. _____ _____ is the amount of time between when an order is placed and when the goods are delivered, also known as delivery time.

3. If a company does not pay their bills on time, they are a poor _____ _____.

4. _____, _____ are common credit terms.

5. A _____ is a guarantee that any defective goods will be replaced at no extra cost.

VOCABULARY

cash flow, *n.*   The amount of cash made by a business during a period of time. Having good cash flow means having enough cash to meet one's debts.

credit risk, *n.*   An evaluation of a customer's potential to pay his or her bills

force majeure, *n.*   A cause or event which neither party has control over such as natural disasters, strikes or war. Thus, either or both parties may be excused from responsibilities stated in a contract such as delivery dates, dates of completion, and so forth.

to get in on the ground floor   To get involved in a business opportunity in the beginning

lag time, *n.*   The time between when a decision is made and when it is carried out, or between when an order is placed and when the goods are delivered

penalty for late delivery   An amount of money to be paid by the seller if he or she fails to deliver goods on time

30 days, 1 percent   Credit terms which specify that payment is due within 30 days and if paid by then a 1 percent discount will be given

warranty, *n.*   A guarantee, especially one given by a seller promising to repair or replace goods if they are defective

TOURISM COMES
TO ZANIR

Development
of a Tourist Resort

CASE SUMMARY

Zanir is a poor African country with a beautiful coastline. The Zanirian Ministry of Commerce has recently been contacted by a German tourist resort developer, Abenteuer Urlaub, GmbH., which made a preliminary inquiry concerning the possibility of developing a tourist resort along the Zanirian coastline. At the present time the tourist industry is undeveloped in Zanir, and the inquiry raised an intense debate at the ministry. Zanir could definitely use the income, but some forces in the government are worried about possible negative side effects such as crime and the cultural and environmental impact. In addition, there is the question of the real profit potential since much of the profits could go to the Germans. The case involves several phases: (1) the Germans' presentation of the project, (2) the Zanirians' decision as to whether they wish to enter into formal negotiations, and (3) formal negotiations. In order to understand the background of this debate it is necessary to understand the present situation in Zanir.

Geography and Climate

Zanir is located on the west coast of Africa, north of the equator and south of Mauritania. Its size—12,000,000 square kilometers—makes it one of the smaller African nations. However, it has a scenic and unspoiled coast line of 50 kilometers.

It has an ideal climate for winter tourism as the dry season is from November to May, with an average temperature along the coast of 30 degrees centigrade. It has a major river, the Zana, which supplies adequate water for the present population, but would not supply enough water for the hotel complex anticipated by Abenteuer Urlaub. In addition, the water would not be free of bacteria and would probably cause nausea and diarrhea among some European tourists.

Demography

The population is 2,000,000 of which 500,000 live in the capital. The remaining population lives in rural areas and is involved in agriculture. The average age is relatively low, 32, and the birth and child mortality rates are high. Life expectancy is low, 57, and health conditions are poor. The only health clinics in the rural areas are run by relief organizations and missionaries.

Religion

Ninety percent of the population is Muslim and 10 percent is Christian.

Commerce

Agriculture employs 75 percent of the population, mainly on small, family farms of one to five acres. There are a few large plantations owned by whites who remained after Zanir's independence from Great Britain in 1980. The peasants are involved in subsistence farming, while the large plantations produce single crops for export. The major export crops are groundnuts, cotton, and rice. Some beef is produced for local consumption. There is 40 percent unemployment, particularly in the capitol which is a magnet for the rural unemployed who gravitate to slums and survive as best they can. The GNP per inhabitant is U.S. $400.

Education

Fifty percent of the population is illiterate. Public schooling is only available to a sixth grade level and attendance levels are low, particularly in the rural areas.

Politics

Zanir is a multiparty state with democratic elections. The president is elected for five years in a direct election. The parliament consists of one house, and its members are also elected for a five-year term. There have been three elections since independence. The first five years the country was run by a self-proclaimed leader who has subsequently been re-elected three times in relatively democratic elections. The political situation in Zanir is considered to be relatively stable. However, economic stagnation, rising unemployment (from 25 percent in 1993 to 40 percent in 1995), increasing budget deficits, and national debt threaten this stability. The lack of hard currency has made it impossible for Zanir to service its loans from the International Monetary Fund (IMF), and representatives of the government are currently meeting with IMF representatives to restructure their loans.

In the Zanirian Ministry of Commerce two opposing forces have emerged. One sees tourism as a possible source of desperately needed hard currency, jobs, and revenues to reduce budget deficits. The other side sees potential dangers to the social structure of Zanir. It warns that tourism will bring prostitution, sexually transmitted diseases, and crime and will break down the traditional family structure by drawing men away from the rural areas, the farms, and their families. In addition, this faction fears that Western values will challenge traditional Muslim values. It is also skeptical about the economic benefits of tourism. It points to another African nation in a similar situation and claims that most of the benefits of tourism go to the European companies. Charter trips are paid for in the country of origin and very little money is spent in the African countries. The limited amount of money spent in the country does not warrant the expenditures on infrastructure necessary to satisfy European tourists' expectations. If the resort is wholly owned by Abenteuer, the payback period to cover the cost of the airport (U.S. $15,000,000), roads (U.S. $3,000,000), and water and sewage systems (U.S. $5,000,000) is calculated to be 15 years, and it is questionable whether procuring this money through loans would be possible given the present economic situation of the country.

Nevertheless, after a lengthy discussion the ministry decided to meet with the representatives of Abenteuer Urlaub to hear their offer. The Zanirian delegation will consist of representatives from both factions. Abenteuer Urlaub has got wind of the split in the delegation through the German embassy in Zanir and is aware of the fact that they will be confronted by some hostile members of the Zanirian delegation who will make demands concerning the following:

1. *Ownership of the resort.* It is standard for Abenteurer Urlaub to own 100 percent of a resort. They buy the property, then construct and own the resort.

2. *Repatriation of profits.* Abenteuer Urlaub has previously retained all profits from operations both in Germany (sales of package trips) and profits generated in the country of the resort.

3. *Expenditures on infrastructure.* Abenteuer usually covers the construction of roads within the resort and sewage treatment facilities. However, roads from the airport and water supply are seen as the responsibility of the government.

4. *Training and hiring of employees.* Abenteuer has always used local residents as menial help (maids, janitors) and service personnel (waiters, bell boys) while hiring Europeans for all reception, reservations, food services, and managerial positions.

CULTURAL BACKGROUND

Two groups will be selected by the teacher to present an analysis of the two cultures of negotiations in this case. For the African team, choose an appropriate country in the geographical region specified in the case. Discuss items mentioned in Chapter 2 on cross-cultural negotiations, such as (1) differing concepts of time, (2) the purpose of negotiations—deal versus relationship establishment, (3) the value and importance of protocol, and so forth, and (4) (not mentioned in Chapter 2) the burden of the colonial relationship between Europe and Africa on present negotiations. After each group has presented its culture, both teams will conclude by pointing out areas where, due to differences in the two cultures of negotiation, misunderstanding, frustration, and conflicts might occur.

QUESTIONS FOR DISCUSSION

1. What historical factors in the relation between European and African countries might make these negotiations difficult?
2. What can the Abenteuer team do to lessen the problems?

CASE

The case will consist of a preliminary meeting where Abenteuer Urlaub will present its proposal and the representatives from the Zanirian Ministry of Commerce will ask specific questions to try to get a better idea of the details.

Then the representatives from the ministry will discuss the initial proposal among themselves and decide whether further negotiations are worthwhile. In the event that they do, they will write a letter inviting Abenteuer for formal negotiations.

The Case Sequence

1. PRE-NEGOTIATION: Each side will prepare for the negotiations by discussing their negotiation strategy and filling out the Negotiations Worksheet and the Position Presentation Worksheet. (Appendices 3 and 4)

2. RECEPTION: There is a certain amount of suspicion built into this negotiation. The Zanirians are skeptical of previous colonial powers and their intentions. They question whether the Germans are simply interested in exploiting the natural beauty of Zanir and repatriating the profits, and they wonder if the Germans realize the possible dangers of the cultural conflicts inherent in such a project. How environmentally conscious are the Germans, and how much have they considered the drain on the Zanirian water supply the proposed project will have? How interested are the Germans in contributing to Zanirian development through training and jobs, technology transfer, infrastructure improvement, and current accounts? Thus, they arrange a reception to get to know the Abenteuer Urlaub delegation and to sound out diplomatically and subtly the German's intentions.

3. **THE FIRST MEETING:** After introductions and some brief socializing where the Abenteuer Urlaub team thanks the Zanirians for the reception, Abenteuer Urlaub will present their concept. Drawings of the intended resort will be presented and the following details will be covered:

    a. *Layout of the Resort and Facilities.* Will there be several high-rise buildings or many bungalows? Will there be a swimming pool, tennis courts, a golf course, infirmary, bars, discos? Presented by Freidrich Beck, Chief Architect.

    b. *Target Market.* What is the intended target market, the "sun and fun" crowd of young singles and couples, families, the elderly? Presented by Uwe Stein, Head of Tourist Product Development.

    c. *Sanitation Facilities.* Does Abenteuer plan to build their own sewage treatment system or connect with the existing system? Presented by Kurt Berg, Chief Engineer.

    d. *Water Consumption.* How many liters of water per day will be consumed by the resort? Will it be tapped from the existing water supply or will the non-drinking water be processed from sea water? Who is expected to pay for the processing plant? Presented by Kurt Berg, Chief Engineer.

    e. *Employment.* How many Zanirian nationals will be hired during the construction period and how many during the operation period? What level will these positions be on and what training will be provided? Presented by Hans Friedl, Comptroller.

    f. *Supplies.* What products will be purchased from local sources, and what will the annual revenues be for these sources? Presented by Hans Friedl, Comptroller.

The Zanirian delegation will ask questions after each segment is presented. Their team consists of: Mr. Abdlai N'Doya, Deputy Secretary of Tourism, who will head the team and ask questions pertaining to layout and facilities, ownership, and operations; Dr. Sidia Sallah, Chief Engineer for the Ministry of Interior, who will raise questions about water, roads, and sanitation; Mr. Koro Jaulara, Deputy Secretary of the Department of Employment, who will ask questions about employment; and Dr. Sankung M'Bye, Deputy Secretary of the Ministry of Agriculture, who will raise questions about the impact on the local farmers, including use of water and the purchasing of farm goods.

The team representing Abenteuer Urlaub will consist of the following persons: Head of Tourist Product Development, Uwe Stein, who heads the delegation; the Chief Engineer, Kurt Berg; the Chief Architect, Freidrich Beck; and the Comptroller, Hans Friedl.

4. THE SECOND MEETING: After the first meeting, the Zanirian delegation will meet to decide if further meetings are appropriate. If the delegation is negative to the project, they will express this in the form of a letter. However, if they wish to explore the possibility further, they will write a letter expressing the desire for a new meeting and set a date. In a letter of rejection, the Minister of Commerce will simply state that the ministry does not consider the project of a nature that serves the best interests of Zanir. A letter inviting Abenteuer to further discussions should set the tone and hint at the ministry's position. Expressions such as "We are looking forward to discussing further details of your project," "We are willing to hear details," or "In spite of some reservations to the original plan, we are willing to meet you for further discussion" suggest various tones which can be established in the letter.

5. THE THIRD MEETING: The Zanirian team will consist of the Permanent Secretary of the Ministry of Commerce, Mr. Koro Jobe, who will head the delegation, and the others who were at the first meeting. The Abenteuer Urlaub team will consist of the Head of Tourist Product Development, Uwe Stein, who will head the delegation, and the others present at the first meeting plus a new member, Marianne Steinberg, the Head of the Legal Division. The meeting will begin with Uwe Stein's introduction of his team to the Permanent Secretary of the Ministry of Commerce, Mr. Koro Jobe, and the new member of his team to the other members of the Zanirian team. Those who were present at the first meeting will exchange pleasantries such as that it is good to see each other again and to be back in their beautiful country, and how nice it is to get away from the bad weather in Germany.

MEETING AGENDA

1. Reservations concerning the project as outlined in the first meeting. Here the Zanirian delegation will present areas of concern in relation to the project as it was outlined in the first meeting and Abenteuer will respond. (Questions that might be raised are the physical layout of the resort, the intended target market—especially if it is the sun and fun crowd, and the amount of food stuffs to be supplied by the local farmers).

2. Ownership of the resort. Will the resort be wholly owned by Abenteuer or will ownership be shared with the Zanirian government?

3. Repatriation of profits. What percentage of the profits coming from the resort can Abenteuer transfer to Germany?

4. The covering of construction costs for the sewage system, a possible sea water conversion plant, and roads within the resort and to and from the airport.

5. Employment and training of Zanirian nationals. How many Zanirians will be hired? What kind of training will they receive? What positions can they hope to obtain in the resort?

If negotiations fail to reach an agreement, tell why.

6. FINAL AGREEMENT: If a final agreement is reached, it will be summarized and then written up in the form of a contract.

7. ANALYSIS OF THE NEGOTIATIONS: Make a presentation where the two teams present the contract arrived at and each team presents its strategy, its goals, and how successful they were in attaining their goals in the contract.

LANGUAGE MASTERY EXERCISES

Written Exercises

1. The Manager of Tourist Product Development at Abenteuer Urlaub, Uwe Stein, will write a letter to the Zanirian Minister of Commerce inquiring about the possibility of a meeting to discuss the development of a tourist resort in Zanir. The letter will generally present the project, including the location (beach front) and approximate size of the land required (1 square kilometer), briefly mention the mutual advantages of the project, and ask for a meeting to present the project in more detail. The tone of the letter is extremely important and must be characterized by formality and respect. Use the following greeting and closing:

   INSIDE ADDRESS: The Honorable Dr. Emanuel N'Komo
   Minister of Commerce

   GREETING: Dear Sir:

   CLOSING: Yours respectfully,

   Use terms such as:

   > We respectfully request ...
   > We believe a tourist development project to be mutually beneficial.
   > We would appreciate your consideration of our request and hope that you may grant us an opportunity to present our concept in detail for your consideration.

2. A member of the Ministry of Commerce, the Deputy Secretary of Tourism, will write a letter in response to Abenteuer's letter and assign a date for the meeting. The letter will be addressed to Uwe Stein.

   GREETING: Dear Mr. Stein:

   CLOSING: Yours sincerely,

3. After the first meeting and after the Ministry has considered Abenteuer's proposal, a member will write a letter accepting or rejecting further negotiations.

4. Fill in the Negotiations Worksheet (see Appendix 3) and the Position Presentation Worksheet (see Appendix 4) as part of the pre-negotiation activities.

Oral Exercises

The first meeting will commence with introductions. It is proper protocol for the head of the Abenteuer team, Uwe Stein, to introduce himself and his team first to the head of the Zanirian team, Mr. N'Doya, Deputy Minister of Tourism, and then the other members of the Zanirian team in order of their rank. Assume for this exercise that N'Doya is sitting at the head of the table and his associates are ranked according to how far they are sitting from him. Stein would first introduce himself to the Deputy Secretary of Tourism and thank him for granting the meeting and taking his and his delegations' time to listen to the concept. In addition, he would compliment the Zanirians on their beautiful country and their hospitality. He would then introduce the other members of his team to Mr. Abdlai N'Doya. Practice introductions such as the one below by Uwe Stein:

> "Mr. N'Doya, as Head of Tourist Product Development at Abenteuer
> Urlaub, I want to thank you for allowing us to meet with you and
> present our ideas. I hope you will consider allowing us to build a
> resort in your beautiful country and that we may enjoy a long and
> mutually beneficial relationship. I would like you to meet the members
> of our delegation. First, our Chief Engineer, Kurt Berg ..."

After Stein has introduced his delegation, N'Doya would thank the Abenteuer delegation for coming and introduce his delegation.

In the second meeting, Stein would introduce his delegation to the Permanent Secretary, Mr. Koro Jobe. Then, he would introduce the new member, Marianne Steinberg, to those present at the first meeting. Those present at the first meeting would express their pleasure at seeing each other again.

The meeting will be chaired by Mr. Koro Jobe, the Permanent Secretary of the Ministry of Commerce. He would open the meeting by saying the following or something similar.

> "Thank you once again for coming. As we expressed in our letter, we
> are interested in the resort project which you have proposed and
> would like to have further details. So may we move on to the items
> on the agenda? Item one concerns ownership. What do you propose?"

After the Abenteuer team presents its position, the real negotiating begins. You will need a full range of expressions which you will find in Appendix 5. Practice the exercises, presenting opinions and agreeing and disagreeing, which you will find in this appendix. Study the expressions and be prepared to use them. Practice the drills in each exercise in pairs consisting of one member from an Abenteuer team and one member from a Zanirian team.

Comparative and Superlative Adjectives

1. Comparative Adjectives

The comparative is used to express differences between two people, places, or things.

> Beaujolais is a *lighter* wine than Burgundy.
> The Ritz is *more expensive* than the Plaza.

Note that there are two forms of the comparative. The *-er* ending is used with one- and two-syllable adjectives (clean, light, heavy). With adjectives of three or more syllables (expensive, luxurious) and multiword adjectives (hardworking, goal minded) use *more + adjective* form.

Complete the sentences using the appropriate comparative form of the adjectives in parentheses.

1. The service at the Plaza is _____ than at the Ritz. (good)

2. The beaches in Zanir are _____ than the beaches in Sendal. (white)

3. Hotels in Zanir would be _____ than hotels in Sendal. (expensive)

4. The receptionists at the Towers hotels are _____ than the receptionists at the Balmore hotels. (friendly)

5. She is _____ than he is. (service minded)

2. Superlative Adjectives

Superlatives are used to compare three or more people, places, or things. There are two forms of the superlative. The *-est* ending is used with one- and two-syllable adjectives, while *most + adjective* is used with adjectives of three syllables or more.

> She is *the best* cook in Paris.
> He is *the friendliest* receptionist I know. (two syllables)
> He is *the most responsible* person at the hotel. (more than two syllables)

Complete the sentences using the appropriate superlative form of the adjectives in parentheses.

1. The Ritz is _____ hotel in town. (expensive)

2. The Towers provides _____ service of any hotel in Zanir. (good)

3. She is _____ assistant I know of. (efficient)

4. They have _____ staff in the chain. (service minded)

5. German white wines are _____ wines in the world. (sweet)

Vocabulary Exercise

Complete these sentences with words and phrases from the vocabulary list.

1. Zanir has many problems. The country has high _____ (many people without jobs) and a poor _____ (communication systems, roads, electricity, and so forth).

2. In addition, the government spends more than the _____ it takes in from taxes. Thus, it is running a _____ each year and the _____ _____ is rising.

3. There are certain advantages to the project, but still the government has _____ due to possible negative effects.

4. If the Germans are allowed 100 percent _____ ____ _____, Zanir will not increase their holding of _____ _____.

VOCABULARY

benefits, *n.*   Advantages

child mortality, *n.*   Death rates among children

concept, *n.*   A business idea

consumption, *n.* **(to consume,** *v.*)   Using up of food, energy, or resources

deficit, *n.*   The negative amount between expenses and income; it occurs when a government spends more than it takes in

demography, *n.*   The study of population distribution, especially births, deaths, age, and sex

desalinization plant, *n.*   A facility which converts sea water into fresh water

to gravitate, *v*   To move toward or be attracted to something

hard currency, *n.*   Currency that is not likely to fall suddenly in value; currency that can be exchanged

illiterate, *adj.*   Not being able to read or write

impact, *n.* **(to impact,** *v.*)   A major effect

infirmary, *n.*   A small hospital

infrastructure, *n.*   Water, power, roads, transport, telephone and radio communication needed to support economic activity

inquiry, *n.*   Request for help or information

national debt, *n.*   The total amount a country owes its creditors

payback period, *n.*   The time required to earn back an investment

peasant, *n.*   Poor farmer

preliminary, *adj.*   Something in preparation to or coming before an event

to push for, *v.*   To urge someone to accept something strongly

repatriation of profits, *n.*   Bringing money earned abroad back to the home country of the company involved

reservations, *n.*   Doubts about a project,which prevent one from supporting it

to restructure, *v.*   To change the payback time schedule of loans for debtors that cannot meet the present schedule due to lack of funds

revenue, *n.*   Income, usually used for governments' income

self-proclaimed, *adj.*   To declare oneself (in this case to appoint oneself as head of the country)

sewage, *n.*   Waste from human beings and industrial sources

subordinate, *n.*   A person of lower rank or position

unemployment, *n.*   The state of not being employed/being out of work

unemployment rate, *n.*   The percentage of those who are able to work but who do not have employment

SMIRNOV GOES
TO PARIS ST. GERMAIN

A Player's Contract

CASE SUMMARY

This case involves the selling, buying and/or renting of football (Br.)/soccer (Am.) players. It involves a multiparty deal between Russia, France, and possibly Italy, England, and The Netherlands. In France, football is not just a sport but in many cases a way of life. Supporter clubs follow their team all around the country, and much of the members' social activities center around the games and related activities. It is not surprising, then, that the team's success or failure is the major item of concern, and when a team's fortune turns for the worse, there is outrage. In addition, there are millions of dollars in circulation to buy new players and their wages have reached incredible levels. Still, no club owner wants to pay more than is necessary and is always looking for good deals. English clubs have discovered that Norwegian players are both good and cheap, while Russian players, due to the economic conditions in their country, are now seen as a bargain. Russian salaries, seen in terms of buying power, have been eroded due to inflation. In addition, attendance at sports events is down in Russia, leaving the clubs no alternative but to sell or hire out some of their best players. However, selling off players can make a bad situation worse because a club's performance impacts on attendance figures.

CULTURAL BACKGROUND

One group will be selected by the teacher to present an analysis of each of the cultures of negotiations in this case—Russia, France, Italy, the Netherlands, and England—along the lines discussed in Chapter 2 on cross-cultural negotiations, such as (1) differing concepts of time, (2) the purpose of negotiations—deal versus relationship establishment, (3) approaches to decision making, and (4) the value and importance of protocol, ceremony, and so forth. After each of the five groups has presented its culture, it will conclude by pointing out areas where, due to differences in its respective culture of negotiation, misunderstanding, frustration, and conflicts might occur.

QUESTIONS FOR DISCUSSION

1. Have football players become commodities? How do you feel about the high prices they bring on the market?
2. Have commercial considerations become more important than the sport itself?
3. What kind of pressures are football players under to perform, given their high salaries, and how does that affect them personally?

CASE

Until recently, 1993, the football club Paris St. Germain has enjoyed great success. However, injuries, internal conflicts, and bad luck have left the club with only six points after five games, and near the bottom of the top division. The fans are calling for the manager's head on a platter and the players are disgruntled. Their top scorer, George Durran, has only scored one goal in five games, and he is demanding a transfer due to conflicts between himself and the manager, Louis La Fontaine. La Fontaine would like to get rid of Durran, who is a "trouble maker" and has been stirring up discontent among the players. Still, if he does get rid of Durran and Durran proves to be the goal getter that he was in the past, La Fontaine would look very bad in the eyes of the fans and the owners. What he needs is a new goal getter whose performance would make the fans forget Durran. He knows that fans have very short memories when a club starts winning and therefore sees a double reason for getting rid of Durran. For one thing, he might get a scoring forward, and second, he would get rid of a source of dissension in the club. He heard about Yuri Smirnov, a top-scoring forward in the Russian club Spartak Moscow, and has sent his scouts to see him play a UEFA Cup match. They came back with a glowing report.

Scouting Report—Yuri Smirnov

Personal data

Age:	24
Height:	183 cm
Weight:	75 kg
Civil Status:	Married with two children, ages 2 years and 6 months

Year	Goals	Assist	Yellow cards	Red cards
1995	22	14	2	0
1994	17	9	4	0
1993	13	7	5	0

Speed: 4.4 seconds for 40 meters

Talent: Not only is Smirnov a well-rounded player who scores both with headers and an incredible right foot, but he is a team player and gives 110 percent for 90 minutes. He has excellent ball control, good overview, and a good sense for open players. Passes are 80 percent successful and his combinations with teammates are daring, inventive, and surprising for the opposition.

Personality: He is very serious, trains hard, is a bit shy, and would have to adjust to media attention. He should be protected from the media in the beginning. He is very controlled and not given to bursts of temper. He is well liked by his teammates and is above all an unselfish team player.

Recommendation: He is exactly what the club needs and with a month's practice could replace Durran, create a better team spirit, and work well with Le Blanc in our 4-4-2 system.

Having read the report, La Fontaine sees the possibility of selling Durran. He has had several inquiries about selling Durran from other clubs, and he could get Smirnov for a fraction of the amount he would get for Durran. As the UEFA Cup match was the last game of the season for Spartak Moscow, they would be willing to release him immediately. Even if they would not be willing to sell him, he could be hired out for the remainder of the French season, which corresponds with the off-season in Russia.

Thus, La Fontaine contacts Smirnov and Spartak Moscow at the same time that he contacts Ajax, Tottenham, and Inter Milan, who have expressed interest in Durran.

Role—The following teams consist of two members:

1. Two representatives from Paris St. Germain to negotiate with Spartak Moscow (two members) and eventually Smirnov and his agent (two members)
2. Two representatives from Paris St. Germain to inquire and eventually negotiate with representatives from Ajax, Tottenham, and Inter Milan
3. Smirnov and his agent
4. Two representatives from Ajax to meet and eventually negotiate with the two representatives from Paris St. Germain
5. Two representatives from Tottenham to meet and eventually negotiate with the two representatives from Paris St. Germain
6. Two representatives from Inter Milan to meet and eventually negotiate with the two representatives from Paris St. Germain

The Case Sequence

Each side will prepare for each phase of the negotiations by discussing their negotiations strategy and filling out the Negotiations Worksheet and the Position Presentation Worksheet. (Appendices 3 and 4)

PHASE ONE

1. The first phase of the case will be divided into two simultaneous negotiations involving the clubs in question.

   Two representatives from the management of Paris St. Germain will contact representatives from Spartak Moscow and attempt to reach agreement on either a transfer (purchase) or rental of Smirnov. They will negotiate a transfer sum (the amount to be paid to Spartak Moscow if they intend to buy Smirnov) or a rental sum (if they intend to rent Smirnov) and the length of the rental (usually one season at a time). In the event of a rental, they should negotiate compensation to be paid Spartak Moscow in the event of injury to Smirnov.

2. Meanwhile, two other representatives of Paris St. Germain will contact Ajax, Tottenham, and Inter Milan and attempt to reach an agreement on either a transfer (purchase) or rental of Durran. No contract will be signed. The Paris St. Germain representatives just want to get an idea about interest and the approximate price for Durran in the event that the deal for Smirnov goes through.

   If an agreement is reached between St. Germain and Spartak Moscow and there is at least one club interested in Durran, proceed to the next phase. If not, the case is finished.

The teams involved in phase one

   a. Paris St. Germain and Spartak Moscow—two representatives from each club
   b. Paris St. Germain—two representatives from Paris St. Germain will meet two representatives from each of the following clubs:
   Tottenham
   Inter Milan
   Ajax

The meetings will occur separately.

   After the first phase, the four representatives from Paris St. Germain will get together to share notes and develop a strategy for the next round. The representatives from Paris St. Germain will be responsible for setting the meeting agenda.

PHASE TWO

The same two representatives from Paris St. Germain who negotiated with Spartak Moscow will meet Smirnov and his agent and negotiate.

MEETING AGENDA

1. Salary
2. Length of contract
3. Fringe benefits: free car, housing, and matters concerning Smirnov's family (day care, job possibilities for his wife, etc.)

PHASE THREE

If Paris St. Germain signs Smirnov, they must reach a deal with one of the clubs interested in Durran. They will negotiate the transfer sum (the amount to be paid to Paris St. Germain) or a rental sum (if they intend to rent out Durran) and the length of the rental (usually one season at a time). In the event of a rental, they should negotiate compensation to be paid to Paris St. Germain in the event of injury to Durran.

 The representatives from Paris St. Germain will be responsible for setting the meeting agenda.

DURRAN AND HIS TRANSFER CLUB

To simplify this case, the negotiations between Durran and either Ajax, Tottenham, or Inter Milan will not be carried out.

LANGUAGE MASTERY EXERCISES

Written Exercises

1. Fill in the Negotiations Worksheet (see Appendix 3) and the Position Presentation Worksheet (see Appendix 4) as part of the pre-negotiation activities.
2. Write an article for the sports section of an English newspaper about the recent problems for Paris St. Germain, their causes, and rumors of trades that the club is involved in.

Oral Exercises

Negotiations such as the ones in this case involve many social activities since the people involved either know each other or know of each other. Thus, one must master social skills and language. After studying the common social phrases that follow, go out to lunch with members of another team with whom you will be negotiating. You can make this realistic by actually going to a restaurant or canteen on campus to carry out this conversation.

INTRODUCTIONS

See the oral exercises in Case 2: "Sansung Sporting Goods Seeks a Scandinavian Distributor."

SEEING PEOPLE AGAIN

Jack: Hello Paul, good to see you again.

Paul: Hello Jack, good to see you.

Jack: How's the club doing? I see that you are in third place.

Paul: Yes, three more matches and we will be on top. What about your prospects?

Jack: Not bad. We are in the middle of the pack, but we've been plagued by injury. But now that everyone's fit, we should start climbing.

BUYING DRINKS

What would you like to drink? *(formal)*

Would you like a drink? *(neutral)*

What are you drinking/having? *(informal)*

Can I get you something to drink? *(neutral)*

SUGGESTING A RESTAURANT

I suggest we go to the La Brochette. They have excellent food and good atmosphere.

ORDERING FOOD

Paul: What can I order for you? *(formal)*

What are you having? *(informal)*

What looks good? *(informal)*

OR

Paul: Jack, if you haven't already made up your mind, I might suggest the Chateaubriand. It's very good.

Jack: That sounds good. Can you recommend a good wine to go with it?

Paul: Yes, they have an excellent Cabernet Sauvignon.

INVITING AND ACCEPTING

Paul: I'd like the pleasure of taking you out to lunch. *(formal)*

I'd like to take you out to lunch. *(neutral)*

Can I take you out to lunch? *(neutral)*

Lunch is on me. *(very informal)*

THANKING AND ACKNOWLEDGING THANKS

Thank you. That's very kind of you. *(formal)*

Thank you very much. *(neutral)*

Thanks. *(informal)*

My pleasure *(slightly formal)*

You're quite welcome. *(neutral)*

You're welcome. *(neutral)*

Think nothing of it. *(informal)*

Don't mention it. *(informal)*

AGREEING AND DISAGREEING INFORMALLY

That's great. *(enthusiastic)*

That's fine. *(less enthusiastic than "That's great," but still positive)*

That's all right. *(neutral)*

That's OK. *(neutral)*

No, I'm afraid not. *(polite and diplomatic)*

I'm not so sure. *(doubt but not definitely no)*

I don't think so. *(polite, but not definitely no)*

Definitely not. *(firm)*

CONCLUDING A CONVERSATION

OK (name), I'll get back to you as soon as I know something definite.

I'll call you in a week.

Good bye and thanks for ...

I'll see you soon.

Asking Questions

In both social situations and in negotiations, you must know how to ask questions. Using the social situations just indicated, ask an appropriate question for the following situations. You have various options.

Polite:	Would you like ...?
More informal:	How about a ...?
	What are you (having)?
	Are you ready to ...?

1. You are going to a restaurant and ask a business associate if he or she has any preference as to what kind of restaurant to go to.

2. You are ready to order and wonder if a business associate is ready to order.

3. You see someone for the first time in a long time. What do you say?

4. You invite someone to a party (asking a question).

5. You meet someone at the airport and ask them about their flight.

6. You question someone's statistics in a diplomatic fashion. Begin with "Excuse me, but ...."

7. Someone makes a totally unacceptable offer. Point this out in a diplomatic fashion, beginning with "I wonder if ..."

8. You need to meet with your team to discuss an offer made by the other team. Ask for a recess in a polite manner, suggesting that both sides could use a break, beginning with "I wonder if ..."

9. Try to get a feeling for the other team's position on renting versus buying Durran.

10. Be direct and try to find out what the other side is willing to pay for Durran.

VOCABULARY

agent, *n.*   A person who represents you in business affairs

commodity, *n.*   A product which can be bought and sold

day care, *n.*   A person or institution that can take care of children during the day while parents are working

CHEMI SUISSE
VS. THE STATE OF INDIA

A Catastrophe
and Claims for Compensation

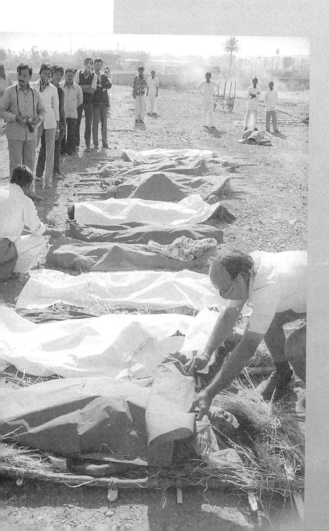

CASE SUMMARY

This case involves claims for compensation after the explosion in a Swiss-owned chemical factory rocks a small Indian town, killing many people. There are serious questions of criminal negligence due to inadequate safety devices and routines on the part of the Swiss company.

European producers have traditionally sought low-cost countries as production sites in order to lower production costs. Low wages and lax enforcement or lack of legislation protecting workers' rights and the environment have been especially appealing to European manufacturers. However, periodic catastrophes have emphasized the danger in the imbalance between European industries' leverage and developing countries' dependency. Officials in developing countries tend to turn a blind eye to enforcement of laws when dealing with Western industries due to the need for jobs, technology, and investment in the infrastructure. Sometimes these officials are caught in the unfortunate position of having to overlook the safety of their own citizens in order to secure them jobs. However, once a catastrophe occurs, they tend to cover themselves by loud outcries and exorbitant demands for compensation. As a European CEO you may find yourself faced with a lawsuit, which can seriously threaten not only the reputation of your company, but its bottom line. You may face fierce attacks from the local press, environmental groups, unions, public officials who are trying to cover themselves, and local courts who feel public indignation and pressure.

In the last 20 years, India has liberalized a previously restrictive investment policy in an attempt to attract technology and capital goods, thus modernizing its industry. It has become one of the world's ten most industrialized countries. Under Mr. V. P. Singh an emphasis was made to develop the rural areas, and thus companies such as Chemi Suisse were encouraged to locate in such areas. India is not only attractive as a low-cost production site, but as a rapidly expanding market with a population of about 900 million people and a large number of highly educated scientists to provide the know-how for industrial advancement.

Job security is also an important consideration. Thus, the Indian worker is ideally suited to be a cog in a productive wheel. That is why Chemi Suisse spent CHF 300 million two years ago, establishing a production facility for the production of chemicals.

CULTURAL BACKGROUND

Two groups will be selected by the teacher to present an analysis of the two cultures of negotiations in this case—India and Switzerland—along the lines discussed in Chapter 2 on cross-cultural negotiations, such as (1) differing concepts of time, (2) the purpose of negotiations—deal versus relationship establishment, (3) approaches to decision making, and (4) the value and importance of protocol, ceremony, and so forth. Another question to be raised is how the Indian negotiators' indignation will affect the negotiations and how the Swiss team should approach the negotiations—that is, what tone should they take. Remember, the Indians have the courts on their side if the case goes that far.

After each group has presented its culture, both teams will conclude by pointing out areas where, due to differences in the two cultures of negotiations, misunderstanding, frustration, and conflicts might occur.

QUESTIONS FOR DISCUSSION

1. What pressures are both sides under that will create problems for these negotiations?
2. Is there any possibility of approaching these negotiations from a win-win perspective?
3. What would you expect the tone of the opening statements to be, due to the above problems?

CASE

Hans Brand, CEO of Chemi Suisse, was sleeping soundly in his luxurious home in a Basel suburb when, as if in a distant fog, a bell was heard ringing. He could not localize it, and his biological clock instinctively told him that nothing should be ringing at that time of night. However, it persisted and he finally perceived that it was the telephone. He groped for the receiver, lifted it, and was met by the excited voice of his plant manager in India, Josef Fringeli, whose words cut through the fog of sleep and brought Brand abruptly back to consciousness. "There has been an explosion and fire in our plant. The fire department and civil defense are on the scene, but the fire is still not under control and there have been considerable toxic gases released. I'm afraid the death toll is going to be high," was the message. Brand 's mind pictured the plant in flames and the gases enveloping the surrounding slum, trapping the residents in their vulnerable hovels. The factory had been placed in the slum area as a cost-cutting measure, and the housing was vulnerable due to inadequate windows and doors. Brand's mind flashed from the hellish scenario to the practical question, "What caused the explosion?" He half feared and half hoped that sabotage, as a result of recent bitter wage negotiations and strikes, might be the answer, an answer that would immediately free them from any demand for compensation. "We are not sure yet," was Fringeli's response, "but as soon as the fire is extinguished, we are going in and investigating and will send you the report." "Send it by courier. We don't want the information getting out if it is our fault," was Brand's reply. "Yes, Mr. Brand; I will keep you posted about all the developments," Fringeli said and hung up.

Brand could not sleep the rest of the night and waited for the 6:00 AM news on DRS 1. All that was reported was what he already knew. At 8:00 AM, he drove to his office, where he received a phone call from Fringeli confirming his worst fears. The death toll was reported to be around 1,000, and the hospitals from the surrounding area reported 3,000 people admitted with severe burns and gas poisoning. Brand called an emergency meeting of the board of directors to discuss a preliminary strategy. By the time all the board members had arrived, the Chemi Suisse stock had plummeted on the Zurich Stock Exchange from an all-time high of CHF 113 to 85. The gains that had resulted from the presentation of the annual report and net profits of CHF 335 million from the year before disappeared in two hours. A press release was issued expressing Chemi Suisse's condolences to the families of the deceased and injured, but no mention of responsibility was made. It stated that Chemi Suisse would naturally undertake a thorough investigation and publish the results as soon as they were available.

Two days later, Fringeli called to say that the fire was completely extinguished and that the investigation team sent from headquarters was going in to try to uncover the cause of the accident. However, the one unit where the explosion occurred was so badly damaged that it was questionable whether the cause could ever be established. It flashed through Brand's mind that that might be best if no responsibility could be assigned to Chemi Suisse, and rumors of sabotage could be circulated as a diversionary measure. His thoughts were interrupted by Fringeli's dire message that 2,234 were dead and approximately 5,000 were severely injured. Brand hoped even more fervently that gross negligence on the part of Chemi Suisse could not be established. "Get me the report as soon as possible," was his response to Fringeli.

The report arrived one week later by courier and the Chemi Suisse team made a public statement that due to extensive damage, no cause of the explosion could be determined. The Indian government made a separate investigation, but their experts could not establish the cause of accident either. However, a press release issued along with the report stated clearly that the Indian government would file a criminal negligence suit against Chemi Suisse. Rumors of the compensation around CHF 1 billion to be demanded by the Indian governments surfaced in connection with the press release, but the Indian government had "no comment" when asked about this figure. Added to the CHF 100 million that it would take to rebuild the factory, such compensation could drive Chemi Suisse into bankruptcy. The debt on the factory alone was CHF 100 million, and potential expenses due to claims for compensation painted a bleak picture.

Roles to be assigned to groups:

1. Management of Chemi Suisse
2. Representatives for the victims of the explosion, consisting of lawyers and representatives chosen from among next of kin of the victims
3. Representatives of the local government
4. Representatives of the national government

The Case Sequence

Each side will prepare for each phase of the negotiations by discussing their negotiation strategy and filling out the Negotiations Worksheet and the Position Presentation Worksheet. (Appendices 3 and 4)

There will be two simultaneous meetings:

1. While representatives of the local and national governments are meeting to settle jurisdiction in this case, representatives from Chemi Suisse will be meeting with representatives of the victims to try to get them to settle immediately. The Chemi Suisse lawyers will promise immediate settlement and are armed with a checkbook and forms. By signing such forms, the victims waive all future claims for compensation.
2. If the victims reject the offer, then the representatives of either the local or national government will meet the representatives of Chemi Suisse out of court to attempt to reach a settlement. If this occurs, both sides must prepare their case.

The Chemi Suisse lawyers should consider the following:

1. The amount of the lump sum compensation for the families of the deceased
2. Disability payments for the injured victims and length of liability. If the disability permanently prevents the victim from returning to full activity, the payments will be until death. If the victim appears capable of returning to full activity, then a time limit should be established for limitation of responsibility to cover future but presently undetectable effects of the poisonous gas.
3. Safety measures to be financed and carried out by Chemi Suisse

If a solution is not reached, then you can consider the case closed as far as the class is concerned since it would then be turned over to the courts. Unlike the sequence of the previous cases, this case is slightly different. If a settlement is not reached between Chemi Suisse and the local residents, the following sequence will be followed for the meeting between Chemi Suisse and the representatives of the Indian interests.

1. PRE-NEGOTIATION: Prepare the items mentioned and complete the Negotiations and Position Presentation Worksheets in Appendices 3 and 4.

2. SOCIALIZING: Due to the nature of the case, there will be no socializing.

3. SITTING DOWN AT THE NEGOTIATING TABLE: The Indian host, either the Minister of Industry, Mr. Rajiv Sathe, or the local governor, Arun Singh, depending on who represents the Indian interests, will be polite but not friendly in assigning seats to the Chemi Swiss team and introducing team members. (Names are provided, but you must determine their title based on whether the local or national authorities are representing the Indian interests.) Then the head of the Swiss delegation, Hans Brand, will introduce his team.

The Indian Team:

Mr. Charan Vajpayee,
Mr. P. V. Chavan
Mr. Patil Sen
Mr. Vasant Bhagat

The Swiss Team:

Josef Fringeli, Plant Manager
Urs Heiniger, Head of the Investigation Team
Renee Schneider, Chief Legal Counsel
Martin Rousseau, Comptroller

4. OPENING STATEMENTS: The head of the Indian delegation will open the meeting by expressing his indignation. He will set a hard line for the negotiations and suggest that the immediate families and surviving victims of Swiss negligence cannot be fully compensated for their suffering. The head of the Swiss delegation, Hans Brand, will counter with his apologies and condolences to the victims, while not admitting responsibility for the accident.

5. OPENING THE NEGOTIATIONS: The head of the Indian team will open with a strong statement of the guilt and negligence on the part of Chemi Suisse. Hans Brand will counter, emphasizing his sorrow at the extent of the tragedy, but emphasizing that gross negligence cannot be proven. He will then give the floor to Urs Heiniger, who will give the results of the investigation.

MEETING AGENDA

1. The amount of the lump sum compensation for the families of the deceased
2. Disability payments for the injured victims and length of liability. If the disability permanently prevents the victim from returning to full activity, the payments will be until death. If the victim appears capable of returning to full activity, then a time limit should be established for limitation of responsibility to cover future but presently undetectable effects of the poison gas.
3. Safety measure to be financed and carried out by Chemi Suisse

6. CONTINUED NEGOTIATIONS: Negotiations will continue until either an agreement is reached or, due to failure in reaching an agreement, the case is turned over to the courts.

7. SUMMING UP: If an agreement is reached, both teams will go through it and summarize it to be sure that they agree on what has been decided.

8. ANALYSIS OF THE NEGOTIATIONS: Make a presentation where the two teams present the contract arrived at and each team presents its strategy, its goals, and how successful they were in attaining their goals in the contract.

LANGUAGE MASTERY EXERCISES

Written Exercises

The Chemi Suisse teams will write the press release mentioned in the case. The Indian government team will write a press release expressing their indignation and response to the catastrophe and a request that the victims or their next of kin do not settle with Chemi Suisse directly.

1. Fill in the Negotiations Worksheet (see Appendix 3) and the Position Presentation Worksheet (see Appendix 4) as part of the pre-negotiation activities.
2. Write an article for the local newspaper explaining your side of the story. If you are Chemi Suisse, express your sadness at the tragedy and explain what you are willing to do for the local community and the victims. If you are the other teams, express your outrage, your demands for compensation from Chemi Suisse, and why you feel they should meet your demands.

Oral Exercises

THREATENING SANCTIONS

In situations which might involve confrontation, the use of threats of sanctions is not unusual. However, those who threaten sanctions must be sure that they have the power to actually impose them. The Indian representatives are in such a situation, and due to their indignation they may likely resort to sanctions. In the following exercise, practice verbal exchanges that involve threats of sanctions.

Form pairs with one representative from a Chemi Suisse team and one from an Indian team. In the first exercise, the Indian representative will open the exchange with a demand and a threatened sanction to be imposed if the demand is not met. She or he will state the hope that it will not be necessary to implement the sanction, but that will depend on the Chemi Suisse representative's response to the demands. The Chemi Suisse representative will respond, and this response will determine the sequence of responses. In the other two exercises, the Chemi Suisse representative will begin with a statement (example: "There is no proof of negligence") that would irritate the Indian representative, who will then decide whether to immediately threaten to impose sanctions or to question the Chemi Suisse representative's statement with, "You honestly do not expect us to believe that/accept that ..." The Chemi Suisse representative's response will determine the sequence of responses. Note the following means of threatening sanctions and use the one(s) you feel are appropriate to the response from the Chemi Suisse representative. The Chemi Suisse representative can choose to moderate their position or to counterattack with a threatened sanction.

Opening statements which suggest that sanctions can be imposed if Chemi Suisse is not cooperative:

> We hope we can avoid having to ...
> We hope that we will not be forced to ...

The Chemi Suisse representative can then set the tone with a response that will determine the sequence of responses.

Statements seeking an acceptable solution as a response to an unacceptable proposal from Chemi Suisse:

> Naturally, we prefer to reach a reasonable situation, but if this is your final position, we will have to ...
> Am I to understand that you are not willing to ... If so, that would leave us no other alternative but to ...

This leaves the door open to the Chemi Suisse representative to make a more acceptable proposal or not.

Presenting a threat of sanctions due to an unacceptable proposal from the Chemi Suisse representative:

In that event, I am afraid that we must ...
You leave us no other alternative but to ...

The Chemi Suisse representative can then counterattack with her or his own threatening sanction.

If you ... (state the Indian threatened sanction), we will ...
If you ... (state the Indian threatened sanction), we may be forced to ...
   (this is slightly weaker)

Helping Verbs

The use of helping verbs (modals) adds subtlety to language which is extremely important in negotiations. In the following exercises you will review the use of *could, would, may,* and *might* and be introduced to other major helping verbs.

The main helping verbs are: *could, would, should/ought to, can, will, shall, might, may, must, to have to.*

- *Could* expresses not only possibility, but is often used in polite requests along with *would.*

     Would/could you help me? *(polite request)*
     I *would* like a room. *(polite request)*
     Would you like some coffee? *(polite offer)*

Could also expresses the past tense of *can.*

     When I was a boy, you *could* go out at night without being afraid.

Could can also be used to suggest an alternative solution.

     You *could* try the hotel across the street. Perhaps they have a vacancy.

- *Would* is also often used to make suggestions.

     I *would* go to Grand.
     I *would* suggest the Lobster Inn.

- *Should* expresses moral obligation or is used to give advice.

     You *should* be kind to your parents. *(moral obligation)*
     You *should* stop smoking. *(advice)*
     You *should* book your plain ticket in advance. *(advice)*

Should also expresses something that you were supposed to do, but didn't.

     We *should* have finished the meeting by 12 noon.

However, something that you planned on doing but didn't is expressed by: "We were going to go to the theater, but changed our minds." "We intended to go/We planned on going."

- *Ought to* is a synonym for *should* but is not often used.

- *Must* expresses something obligatory. There is no past tense of must and you must use *had to* the the past tense equivalent of *have to* .

    We *had to* work until midnight.

    For the future, you have a choice: "We must/have to/will have to work all day tomorrow."

- *May* expresses both a polite request and a possibility.

    May I borrow your car?
    He *may not* be well enough to work tomorrow.

    A synonym that you can use to express possibility is *might*. *Might* can also be used to give advice. "You might consider being more friendly."

- *Will* is used more in written than in spoken English. In spoken English, the present continuous ("I am working tomorrow.") is more often used instead of *will* to express future. *Will* is often used to indicate a factual occurrence in the future, or for emphasis.

    The train *will be* here at 7 PM. *(factual occurrence)*
    You ***will*** do it. *(heavy emphasis on the word "will")*

- *Shall* is rarely used except in emphatic sentences or in legal documents.

    You *shall* be here at 5:00. *(emphatic statement)*

Write sentences using modals to express the following meaning.

1. Make a polite request.
2. Make a polite offer.
3. Give some advice.
4. State something obligatory in the present.
5. State something obligatory in the past.
6. State something possible, but not definite.
7. Make a suggestion.
8. Tell about some future event at a definite time.
9. Tell about something that was possible in the past.
10. State something obligatory in the future.
11. Suggest an alternative solution.

Vocabulary Exercise

Use words and phrases from the vocabulary list to complete the sentences.

1. Hans Brand is the _____ of Chemi Suisse.

2. Their _____ security routines were probably a contributing

   cause of the explosion. Their routines were definitely _____.

3. The Indian government is bringing a _____ claiming

   _____   _____.

4. Brand feels that the Indian government's demands are _____.

5. The team's _____   _____ was CHF 500,000. They
   weren't willing to go lower.

VOCABULARY

biological clock, *n.*   An internal sense one has of what time it is

bottom line, *n.*   The lowest you are willing to go to reach an agreement;
the bottom line in a financial report showing profit or loss

capital goods, *n.*   All goods made with the intention of using them to
make other goods

CEO, *n.*   Chief Executive Officer, the head of a company

diversionary, *adj.*   A tactical move to draw an opponent's attention
away from a more important issue

DRS 1, *n.*   A Swiss radio station

enforcement, *n.*   Putting a law into practice; making people abide by laws

exorbitant, *adj.*   Much too high prices or extreme demands

gross negligence, *n.*   An extreme case of failing to perform a duty.
In this case, failing to secure the workers' and local residents' safety

hovel, *n.*   A small house that is almost unfit to live in

inadequate, *adj.*   Not sufficient

lax, *adj.*   Not sufficiently strict

leverage, *n.*   Having an advantage due to power

suburb, *n.*   A residential area outside of a larger town

suit, a lawsuit, *n.*   A case in court involving legal action

to turn a blind eye, *v.*   To pretend not to notice

vulnerable, *adj.*   Unprotected

KENJI MOTORS AND AMERICAN AUTO CORPORATION

A Joint Venture

CASE SUMMARY

Over the past two decades, American and Japanese companies have often found it more profitable to cooperate than to compete. This involves forming a joint venture and working out a joint venture contract, which is the focus of this case. Joint ventures are formed so that the new company can enjoy the synergy effect deriving from the advantages of the two parent companies. In this case, the Japanese company would gain low-cost access to the vast American market and reduced shipping costs, while the American company would gain knowledge of successful production, logistics, quality control, and management techniques. They could cite the old adage, "if you can't beat them, join them." However, joint ventures, especially across cultural boundaries, can lead to conflicts arising from differences in organizational culture. In this case, labor-management relations could be a major source of misunderstanding and conflict. Japanese managers could expect company loyalty and dedication far beyond what is usual in American companies, and these expectations would be irritating for American workers. In addition, the Japanese would have to get used to combative American unions and their negotiating practices. On a personal level, Americans might seem assertive to the point of being considered aggressive and disrespectful, and traditional Japanese deference toward age and authority would probably not be common practice among Americans. The Japanese, who have often criticized American workers as being lazy, would suddenly be dependent on a good working relationship with them. Finally, Japanese success has led to a certain anti-Japanese sentiment in the United States, although unjustly so. The differences in culture will be reflected in their different approaches to negotiations, which should be clarified in detail in the cultural background exercise.

CULTURAL BACKGROUND

Two groups will be selected by the teacher to present an analysis of the two cultures of negotiations in this case—Japan and the United States—along the lines discussed in Chapter 2 on cross-cultural negotiations, such as (1) differing concepts of time, (2) the purpose of negotiations—deal versus relationship establishment, (3) approaches to decision making, and (4) the value and importance of protocol, ceremony, and so forth. After each group has presented its culture, both teams will conclude by pointing out areas where, due to differences in the two cultures of negotiations, misunderstanding, frustration, and conflicts might occur.

This exercise is extremely important because differences in their two cultures of negotiations have created significant problems in negotiations between the Americans and the Japanese.

QUESTIONS FOR DISCUSSION

1. How does the Japanese emphasis on following a strict code of behavior, not only for themselves but for their counterparts, create problems for their counterparts in a negotiation situation? How does this give the Japanese a home court advantage even when negotiating abroad?

2. Given the Japanese expectations that their rules be followed, should a foreign team adjust their behavior or not? If so, in which areas, for example, greater emphasis on protocol and socializing, consensus decision making, emphasizing relationship building over a deal orientation, or others?

3. What major differences will probably cause the greatest misunderstanding, frustration, and conflict?

CASE

This case is a reflection of a common occurrence. Japanese and American companies have formed numerous joint ventures to capitalize on the strengths both sides have to offer. However, negotiations have often been difficult for reasons which you will have explained in the cultural background exercise. This case will help you develop sensitivity toward a culture whose approach to negotiations may be very foreign to yours. Try to get inside your role so as to develop a sensitivity to different approaches, not only in playing your role, but in providing your counterparts with a role that may be foreign to them.

The Case Sequence

1. Pre-Negotiation: The following sequence of events has occurred previous to your negotiations. (1) The CEOs of both corporations met in the United States, where they discussed the general concept of a joint venture agreement. (2) Two months later they agreed to undertake a feasibility study. (3) The feasibility study concluded that a joint venture to produce a Japanese model car in a U. S. plant would be mutually beneficial. (4) The American CEO invited representatives of the Japanese corporation to a meeting in Hawaii, and the Japanese accepted.

Each side will prepare for negotiations by discussing their negotiation strategy and filling out the Negotiations Worksheet and the Position Presentation Worksheet. (Appendices 3 and 4)

Items to be negotiated are:
1. Number and location of the plant(s)
2. Number of cars to be produced
3. The model of the car to be produced—compact or subcompact. You can use actual models and get brochures to illustrate which models you are considering.
4. The licensing fee to be paid to Kenji Motors for use of their car design
5. Ownership of the joint venture
6. Supplying of parts
7. Control of production at the plant, including design of the plant, employee training, quality control, and hiring and firing practices
8. Control of marketing, sales, and distribution

2. SOCIALIZING: As you have undoubtedly discussed, socializing is an important part of the negotiation process. In this case, socializing *should not* involve any discussion of business and should revolve around the visiting team's trip, their satisfaction with the hotel where they are staying, the possibility of getting in a round or two of golf, their golf handicap and favorite courses, their family, and so forth. The setting, Hawaii, has been purposely chosen to create a relaxed, social atmosphere.

3. SITTING DOWN AT THE NEGOTIATING TABLE: The American host team leader, John Smith, Director of Worldwide Product Planning, will place the Japanese on the appropriate side of the table with their head of delegation in the most comfortable seat, furthest from the door (the seat of honor). While still standing, John Smith will present his team members, giving their names and titles. Then Kenji's Head of Overseas Operations, Eiji Sano, will introduce his team members and give their names and titles.

The American Team:

William Frank, Treasurer
Mary Wallace, Corporate Counsel
Robert Daniels, Chief Engineer for Developmental Projects
Ken Hashimoto, Sales Director
Penny Wilson, Executive Secretary to John Smith

The Japanese Team:

Aiko Yamamoto, Treasurer

Masao Koyama, Corporate Counsel

Goro Toyoda, Chief Engineer for Factory and Production Development

Yoshi Takata, Sales Director for Overseas Operations

Minji Yamura, Executive Secretary to Eijo Sano

4. OPENING STATEMENTS: The head of each team will make a statement of welcome (the American team) and appreciation for the invitation (the Japanese team) and their hopes about a mutually satisfying meeting. (See the opening statement suggestions in Case 2, "Sansung Sporting Goods Seeks a Scandinavian Distributor".)

5. OPENING THE NEGOTIATIONS: The head of the American team will open the negotiations by saying something such as: "Let us proceed, then" and suggest the market potential for the new model and the mutual advantages of the joint venture. Naturally, the object is to show that successful negotiations will be profitable for both sides and thus create a positive atmosphere of mutual benefit. The head of the American team will then suggest which point the two teams should discuss first by stating, "I suggest we begin with point one, the number and location(s) of the plants, if you do not have any objections." He should allow time for any objections.

MEETING AGENDA

1. Number and location of the plant(s). American Auto Corporation has two factories that are currently not in use, one outside of San Francisco, California, which is ten years old and one in Ypsilanti, Michigan, which is twenty years old.
2. Number of cars to be produced
3. The model of the car to be produced—compact or subcompact. You can use actual models and get brochures to illustrate the models to which you are referring.
4. The licensing fee to be paid to Kenji Motors for use of their car design
5. Ownership of the joint venture
6. Supplying of parts. Both corporations have their suppliers for batteries, glass, seats, tires, and shock absorbers and will present figures on price and quality control.
7. Control of production at the plant, including design of the plant, employee training, quality control, and hiring and firing practices.
8. Control of marketing, sales, and distribution

Note: Americans tend to progress sequentially, moving from item one to item two, etc. Japanese do not usually move sequentially and may wish to leave an item unfinished and move to another item, especially when there is difficulty in reaching agreement on an item. The American team may wish to rearrange the items on the agenda for tactical purposes. Therefore, do not consider this agenda as fixed. The American team will present a written copy of the agenda at the start of the meeting for approval by the Japanese team.

6. CONTINUED NEGOTIATIONS: Negotiations will continue until one or both of the sides feel a need for a break, either to discuss business separately, contact someone at the head office, or simply to get some fresh air. In the latter case, the two teams can socialize outside of the negotiating room, but remember, this is also part of the negotiation process and relevant information can be subtly exchanged. This could be made realistic by going out to lunch or dinner together. Periodically, throughout the negotiations, particularly when some form of agreement is reached, each team should sum up their understanding of the agreement to avoid misunderstanding.

7. FINAL AGREEMENT: When a final agreement is reached, it will be summarized to ensure that there is no misunderstanding.

8. ANALYSIS OF THE NEGOTIATIONS: Make a presentation where the two teams present the contract arrived at and each team presents its strategy, its goals, and how successful they were in attaining their goals in the contract.

LANGUAGE MASTERY EXERCISES

Written Exercises

1. Fill in the Negotiations Worksheet (see Appendix 3) and the Position Presentation Worksheet (see Appendix 4) as part of the pre-negotiation activities.
2. Each student should keep a notebook of reactions to the other side's negotiation style. Notes should include what they found to be unacceptable, confusing, or frustrating behavior and how they reacted to it and why. This should be done stage by stage so that they can write a sequential analysis. Each group should write up their notes and hand them in as a report entitled "Areas of Differences in Japanese-American Negotiations."

Oral Exercises

Study the section on formal presentation, opening statements, asking questions, asking for clarification, and summing up in Case 2, "Sansung Sporting Goods Seeks a Scandinavian Distributor" as they will be used in this case.

In pairs, practice the exercises "establishing tone," "avoiding locked-in positions by exploring alternatives," and "softening confrontational statements" in Appendix 5.

Adjectives and Adverbs

One final aspect of English that you should master to show your sophistication is an understanding of the difference between adjectives and adverbs, which the following exercise will help you develop. Adjectives and adverbs are often confused even by native speakers. Adjectives describe nouns, whereas adverbs describe verbs of action and adjectives and express frequency and time.

Adjectives	*Adverbs*
He is a *good* worker. ("good" describes the noun "worker")	He works *well*. ("well" describes the verb "work")
He is *active*. ("active" describes "he") The verb *to be* does not describe an action and thus we do not use an adverb. Remember, adverbs are used to describe verbs of action.	He participates *actively*. ("actively" describes the verb of action "participate")

1. Adjectives

Adjectives are used to describe verbs expressing the senses—taste, smell, sound, feel, and look. Thus, you say "the food tastes good," describing the taste of the food. "He looks good" describes his appearance." If you say "He looks well," you are saying that he does not look sick.

2. Adverbs

  a. Adverbs describe adjectives.

   He is *highly* intelligent. ("Intelligent" is an adjective describing
      "He" and "highly" describes "intelligent.")

  b. Adverbs are used to describe frequency and time.

   He eats here *regularly*. *(frequency)*
   Recently, business has been good. *(time)*

   Here are some other adverbs of frequency: *never, rarely, sometimes, often,* and *frequently.*

  c. Most adverbs are formed by taking the adjective and adding *-ly*. Three
     main exceptions are *well, hard,* and *fast*. The word *hardly* exists, but
     it means "almost not at all."

   He works *hard*.
   He runs *fast*.
   It works *well*.

Complete the sentences with the proper form of the word in parentheses—
either the adjective form or the adverb form.

1. The Japanese work _____. (hard)

2. A joint venture can be a _____ arrangement. (profitable)

3. He felt that the deal was _____ worth the effort. (hard)

4. The American team felt that they _____ achieved their goals. (complete)

5. The Japanese factory was _____ run. (good)

6. The Japanese workers were _____ trained. (high)

7. The competition was _____. (tough)

8. They knew the routines _____. (thorough)

9. The deal looks _____. (good)

10. Their victory smelled _____. (sweet)

Vocabulary Exercise

Use words and phrases from the vocabulary list to complete the sentences.

1. The Japanese developed the popular form of logistics known as

   _____-_____-_____ delivery.

2. Due to excellent quality control, Japanese cars have a low

   _____ _____.

3. There are great differences in the way Japanese and American companies

   do business, which are reflected in their different _____

   _____.

4. They conducted a _____ _____ to see
   if there was a market for their new product.

5. _____ _____ can lead to conflicts due to
   differences in organizational cultures.

VOCABULARY

adage, *n.*   A traditional saying

adamant, *adj.*   Firmly determined

CEO, *n.*   Chief Executive Officer, the head of a company

consensus decision making, *n.*   Arriving at decisions through group discussion where the outcome is group agreement

deference, *n.*   Giving way to others' views out of respect for their age and/or position

home court advantage, *n.*   The advantage a team has in playing a game on their home court/field

joint venture, *n.*   A partnership of two or more persons or companies cooperating in some business activity. The partners share the costs and profits in agreed proportions.

just-in-time delivery, *n.*   Organizing logistics so that the supplies are ready when needed, thus saving storage costs

logistics, *n.*   The organization of supplies and services

market survey, *n.*   An analysis of the market potential for a particular product

organizational culture, *n.*   The values, goals, methods, and ways of operating of a specific organization

recall percentage, *n.*   The percentage of units recalled due to errors in production

synergy, *n.*   The advantages derived by merging two organization

GROUP PRESENTATION

An Open-Ended Case

CASE SUMMARY

As stated in Case 5, "Hydra Tech and Bertoni Shipping," presenting your product and showing how much a potential customer needs it is an important part of the negotiating process. The presentation is often made by a group representing a company.

The purpose of this case is to help you develop group presentation skills. To make it realistic, it is an open-ended case, where you have to supply the details, structure the presentation, and ask and answer questions after the presentation. The basis of establishing a strong negotiating position in sales is making your product attractive. A good sales presentation involves several aspects. First and foremost you must remember that you are not only selling a product, but you are providing a solution to the customer's problem and/or satisfying a customer's needs. Thus, the presentation should focus on those needs and each segment of the presentation should emphasize how the product will satisfy those needs. You must establish in the introduction that you understand the customer's problems and needs so as to capture their interest and then address these needs throughout your presentation. The information that follows will provide guidelines for making a good group presentation.

CASE

For this presentation, both teams (buyer and seller) will decide on a situation and establish the buyer's needs. For example, a company needs a computer system to aid in shipping their products. The buyer group will then decide what their specific needs are and convey them to the seller group. The groups will then choose a real product to satisfy those needs, get brochures on that product, and prepare for the presentation. The seller group will prepare a presentation of the product, while the buyer group will prepare questions about the product, price, delivery, service, and so forth. Naturally, the presentation and questions will depend on the product chosen.

The emphasis of this case is on developing presentation technique, and thus the case will not necessarily include negotiations. However, in the question and answer period, questions about price, delivery, service, etc., which would have been part of a negotiation, can be raised. If the class wishes, they can proceed to negotiations, in which case you will have to structure them yourself based on the presentation and the questions and answers.

Making a Good Presentation

INTRODUCTION (OF THE GROUP AND THE TOPIC)

- First and most important is to get your customers' attention. One sure way is to say both what you perceive their needs to be and how your product can solve them. For example, "We are here to save you 20 percent on your current shipping costs, and we will show you how our revolutionary Expedite 80 System can do this by (1) ..., (2) ..., and (3) .... Our analysis of your situation has revealed three main needs which are (1) ..., (2) ..., (3) .... Is that correct?" This question gets the audience involved in the presentation.

- Second, outline your subtopics (product description, advantages over the competitors' products, price, etc.) and introduce the members of your team by name and title and what subtopic they will present. This can be written on an overhead to help the audience systematize your presentation in their minds so that they start to anticipate the organization and thus systematize the information that you are going to present.

- Your introduction of the group should also emphasize the expertise of each of the presenters to encourage confidence and grab the the interest of the audience. For example "Our logistics expert, Tom Smith, will discuss how the Expedite 80 System speeds the flow of parcels up to 20 percent faster than our competitors' models. Tom has a degree in logistics from MIT and was instrumental in developing this system." Your anchorperson, the person who makes the introduction and introduces each speaker, can wind up the introduction by saying: "So how can we save you 20 percent on your shipping costs and solve your three basic problems, (1) ..., (2) ..., and (3) ...? Tom will now explain how the system works and why it is more efficient. Tom."

THE BODY

- This is the main part of the presentation, where the information is given. The key rule is to link all information to the customer's problem and needs. At the same time, you wish to keep the audience involved, which you can do by asking detailed questions about the nature of their needs and then showing how your product will satisfy those needs.

- The anchorperson will introduce each new speaker, their expertise, and topic.

The Conclusion

The anchorperson summarizes the customer's needs and how the product will satisfy them, then asks for questions.

Questions and Answers

The anchorperson refers each question to the appropriate person on his team by saying: "Tom, can you answer that question?" or "I think Tom can answer that question." If some other member of the team wants to add something, they can say, "Excuse me, but I would like to add ...."

Language

Adapt the language to your audience. The more they know about the product, the more technical your language can be. The less they know, the simpler the language should be and the more examples and illustrations should be used. Choosing the proper level of language is extremely important. If you choose language that is too simple, your audience will feel that you are speaking down to them, whereas a too technical language will leave your audience confused.

Voice

Speak loudly and clearly and at a moderate pace. Pause periodically to give the audience a chance to digest what you have said. Be enthusiastic, and do not speak in a monotone. The quality of your voice will reveal how enthusiastic you are about your product. If you are not enthusiastic, why should the audience be?

Maintaining the Audience's Attention

- Ask questions.
- Try to get a dialogue going by focusing on the audience's needs and showing how your product satisfies those needs.
- Emphasize important points by introducing them with "This is important" and then pausing to allow them to focus their attention.

Use of Visuals

Studies have shown that the more an audience sees, the more they will remember of a presentation. Thus, overheads, flip charts, and videos are extremely important. One member of the team can operate the overhead or video machine while the other is talking. This will result in a smoother presentation. Know the size of the room to decide which font to use on your overheads. There is no point in making them if no one can read them. Limit the information on the overheads to key words and figures. Too much information will be counterproductive. Overheads should be removed as soon as you are finished with the information on them and the overhead machine should be turned off unless you are going to use it within 15 seconds. If you have handouts, do not hand them out while you are speaking—they will distract the audience. Hand them out at the end of your presentation.

Body Language

- Eye contact is extremely important. Remember to scan your audience so that they think you are speaking to all of them. When using overheads, do not speak to the screen. Glance at the overhead on the machine if you must, but then lift your eyes and focus on the audience. Do not read your notes, but use them as an outline. If possible, have limited notes and not a manuscript.
- Stand erect and never sit. Do not stand next to a window.
- Lean a bit forward and do not sway back and forth.
- Do not have both hands in your pockets. One hand might be acceptable, but you want to use one hand to make gestures, primarily to emphasize points. Do not overdo hand gestures.
- If you move, do not move too much or move back and forth in the same plane.
- Do not fiddle with things in your hand, such as a pen or your notes. If you are a "fiddler," try not to have anything in your hands. Remember, you can always have your notes on an overhead.
- Smile to show that you are enjoying making the presentation.

Structure your presentation by using the following expressions:

Greetings

Good morning

Good afternoon

Good evening

Introduction of the Group and the Topic

Each group should choose an anchorperson who introduces the group and subject and provides a conclusion. This person can also make part of the presentation, depending on the number of members in the group.

We represent Expedite Systems, Inc. and are going to present a solution to your shipping problems that will save you 20 percent. Our group consists of Eva, who will present a brief introduction of our company; Tom, who will explain the Expedite 80 System; and Roberta, who will cover price; and myself, Alice. I will act as a moderator.

As I have outlined, we will show you how our Expedite 80 System will address the problems you have suggested, that is (1) ..., (2) ..., (3) ..., and show you how you can both solve these problems and save 20 percent on your current shipping costs.

First, Eva will present a brief overview of our company. Eva has been with the company for 15 years and knows all there is to know about its development. Eva. (Eva should then step forward, say "Thank you, Alice," and begin her presentation.)

OPENING STATEMENTS

> Let me begin by saying …
>
> I would like to begin by …

CHANGING THE SUBJECT

> Now that we have looked at our various products, let us look at the
> Expedite 80 System, which we feel is best suited to solve your
> shipping problems.

Note: To make smooth transitions, use sequencing words such as: *first, second, third,* or *first, next, then.* In addition, use transition expressions such as the following:

For comparison

In addition
Equally important
Furthermore

For contrast

On the other hand
However
In spite of/despite
Although

To show cause and effect

Thus
Therefore
Consequently
As a result

HIGHLIGHTS

> Most important, …
> What you must remember, …
> Interestingly enough, …

CONCLUSION

> In conclusion, …
> In summary, …

Appendix 1
BUSINESS
WRITING

FORMAT

Letters

There are three basic letter formats used: (1) *block style,* in which all the lines begin at the left-hand margin; (2) *modified block style,* in which the dateline, the return-address heading, the complimentary close, and the sender's name and title at the end begin in the center of the page; and (3) *indented* (also called *modified block with paragraph indentations*), in which each first line of a new paragraph is indented five spaces and the sender's address and date are placed on the upper right-hand side of the page. Figures A-1 through A-3 give you examples of all three styles of letter.

Note that the first letter, from Miguel Fuentes, uses closed punctuation typical of American correspondence. This means that commas are used after the greeting and closing and that there is a comma between the date and the year. The second letter, from Uwe Stein, uses punctuation typical of the British correspondence style with no punctuation after the greeting and closing and no comma in the dateline. Note also the different order of the dates in American versus British writing.

The underlined sentences and phrases in the letters are part of the tone exercise described on page 135.

Hotel de la Playa
Avenida de la Playa 108
SP-03080 Alicante
Spain

October 23, 199_

Ms. Margaret Smith, Director of Tour Operations
Sun and Fun Tours
25 Hammersmith Road
Harlow, Essex CM19 5AA
England

Dear Ms. Smith,

RE: Delays in Completion of Construction at Hotel de la Playa

We have recently been informed by our contractor that he will
not be able to meet his promised schedule for completion of the
modernization of our hotel. We deeply regret this occurrence for
both our guests' and your sake. We wish that there was something
that could be done, but the causes of this unfortunate event are
outside of our control. A combination of inclement weather and a
strike have delayed completion of the repairs. Naturally, we will
do our utmost to limit the impact of this work on our guests,
and I can assure you that we will pressure the contractors to
complete the work as soon as possible. Realistically, however, we
cannot expect the work to be completed until the end of January.

As both our interests are to ensure that our guests enjoy their
vacation, I would appreciate it if you could contact me so that
we can coordinate our efforts to achieve this goal.

Sincerely,

Miguel Fuentes

Miguel Fuentes, Manager

Figure A-1 Block Style Letter

This is the standard form in Britain, Europe, South America, Australia, and New
Zealand.

```
                                        Abenteuer Urlaub, GmbH
                                        Kaiser Str. 190
                                        D-60437 Frankfurt
                                        Germany

                                        24 October 199_


The Honorable Dr. Emanuel N'Komo
Minister of Commerce
Ministry Building
Zanira
Zanir


Dear Sir

I am writing this inquiry in hopes that we can establish a relation-
ship that will be of benefit to your beautiful country and to our
guests, who would enjoy staying in such beautiful surroundings.
While on a visit to your neighboring country, Mandika, I had the
opportunity to spend several days in your country. I inquired about
tourist facilities and discovered that they were yet undeveloped.
Naturally, I thought that your country could certainly benefit from
the popularity that its beauty would create among potential tourists
and the income that they would bring.

Abentuer Urlaub has established several holiday resorts in Africa
with great benefit to the host countries in terms of job creation
and revenue generation. There is great potential in both of these
areas for a country with such natural beauty as yours. I would thus
appreciate the opportunity to present our concept to your ministry
in hopes that we can establish a mutually beneficial business
relationship.

I look forward to hearing from you and having the possibility of
presenting our ideas.

                                        Yours faithfully
                                        Uwe Stein
                                        Uwe Stein,
                                        Manager,
                                        Tourist Product Development
```

Figure A-2 Modified Block Style Letter

```
                          Ministry of Commerce
                          The State of India
                          Udyod Bhawan
                          New Dehli 110011
                          India

                          February 13, 199_



Mr. Hans Brand
Chemi Suisse
Hauptbahnstr. 23
Ch-4000 Basel
Switzerland

Dear Sir:

    The recent tragedy has raised the question of your company's
concern for the life and health of our people. There can be no
other explanation than gross negligence and total unconcern. When
we originally established our business relationship, you assured me
that everything would be done to ensure that such a tragedy, which
has now occurred, would not occur. It appears that you did not
even install an early warning system in our plant, as you have
done in your Swiss plant. I can only interpret this as a total
disregard for our people and a denial of everything we were
promised during our original negotiations.

    I cannot describe the suffering that your company's negligence
has caused the local population and the effects this negligence
will have for generations. We expect that the people involved be
compensated for their suffering. The Indian government will hold
you totally responsible for the suffering and damage, which is a
result of your negligence. Furthermore, our lawyers will contact
you in the course of next month.

                          Yours faithfully,

                          S. M. Singh

                          S. M. Singh,
                          Minister of Commerce
```

Figure A-3 Indented Style Letter

This is the standard form used in India, Canada, the United States, and Africa.

Letterheads and Return-Address Heading

Most business letters are typed on stationery with a letterhead, that is, with a printed name and address of an organization, company, or business. Thus, the placement of the sender's address usually will be predetermined. If you are using letterhead, you need to add only the date.

If there is no letterhead, place your return-address heading (which gives your address but not your name) at least an inch from the top of the page. In the block style letter, the lines of the return-address heading align at the left margin. In the modified block style letter and indented style letter, the lines fall to the right of the center of the page. Alignment is still on the left.

Dateline

American: May 22, 1995

Britain: 22 May 1995

People in Europe, Africa, Australia, New Zealand, and South America generally use the British dateline. Canadians tend to use both.

Inside Address

This shows the name, title, and address of the person you are writing to. Place this information anywhere from three to twelve lines below the date, depending on the length of your letter. The shorter the letter, the more space there should be between the date and the inside address. In all three styles of letters, the inside address falls at the left margin of the page. You also have to make sure that the spelling of the name of the person receiving your letter, as well as his or her title and address are correct.

Salutations

Salutation greets the addressee. In all three styles it falls at the left margin, two lines below the inside address and two lines above the body of the letter. It is followed by a comma, a colon, or no punctuation (*British style*). For a man, the standard salutation is *Dear Mr.* For a woman, the tendency is to use *Ms.* since it avoids the question of whether the person is married (*Mrs.*) or unmarried (*Miss*). If you are addressing someone whose name or gender you don't know, use *Dear Sir or Dear Madam.*

Subject Line

Many business letters begin with *RE:*, or *SUBJECT,* which states what the letter is going to be about. This gives information without first having to read the entire letter. It is placed two spaces below the salutation and two spaces above the body of the letter. (See Figure A-1.)

The Body

The body of the letter, containing its substance, aligns on the left in all three styles of letters. However, instead of indenting the first line of each paragraph, as in the indented style letter, place an extra line of space between paragraphs.

Complementary Closings

The closing of a letter starts two lines below the last line of the body and aligns with the return-address heading. In the block style it aligns at the left margin (Figure A-1); in the modified block style and indented style letters it falls to the right of the center of the page, but alignment is still on the left. (Figures A-2 and A-3)

The closings can be characterized by their degree of formality. Notice that only the first word of the closing is capitalized, and it is followed by a comma, typical of American correspondence. In British style correspondence there is no punctuation following the closing.

1. *Less formal:* Sincerely, Sincerely yours, Yours sincerely
   These are the standard closings for an American business letter.

2. *More formal:* Respectfully yours, Yours respectfully, Yours truly
   The British tend to be more formal and thus use these complimentary
   closings more often than Americans do. These are also standard closings
   for letters beginning with *Dear Sir, Dear Madam,* or *Dear Sir or Madam.*

Signature

The signature of a business letter follows the closing. It consists of your typed name (the fourth line below the closing phrase) and your handwritten signature (only your name, not your title) is between the closing and the typed name.

REPORTS

Because there are so many types of reports, it is not possible to deal fully with the subject of reports in this section. Instead, this section will give you a brief introduction to format in report writing.

Title Page

A sample title page of a report is shown in Figure A-4.

```
REPORT ON NEGOTIATIONS BETWEEN SSGI AND SANSUNG


       Compiled by the SSGI Negotiations Team
            Jacob Hansen, Sales Manager
           Ole Jensen, Marketing Manager
          Merette Damsgaard, Secretary

























                    July 22, 199_
```

Figure A-4 Report Title Page

Executive Summary

This is a brief description of the contents of the report to allow a reader to know if the report is relevant to his or her purposes without having to read the entire report. It should be typed on a separate page. An example from the report on the negotiations between SSGI and Sansung would be as follows:

```
                    EXECUTIVE  SUMMARY

On July 15, 199_, formal negotiations with Sansung were held
to discuss terms of an eventual contract to distribute Sansung
fishing equipment. This report presents the pre-negotiations
segment, SSGI's goals and strategies, an assessment of the
financial benefits of distributing Sansung fishing equipment,
the negotiation process, the resulting contract, and our
assessment of the contract and recommendation on whether to
accept it.
```

Figure A-5 Executive Summary

Table of Contents

This is placed after the summary. It is prepared after the report is completed and lists in order the numbers and titles of the sections or chapters in the report and the pages on which they begin. In numbering, you have a choice between the American style shown in Figure A-6 or the British system shown in Figure A-7. The table of contents should be typed on a separate page.

```
III.   GOALS
         A. Our Goals
            1.  Musts
            2.  Trading Cards
            3.  The Bottom Line
```

Figure A-6 Table of Contents, American-Style

Note that the American style table of contents uses Roman numerals, capital letters, and cardinal numbers.

```
                    TABLE OF CONTENTS


TITLE PAGE                                              (i)

TABLE OF CONTENTS                                       (ii)

1.0    EXECUTIVE SUMMARY                                 1

2.0    INTRODUCTION                                      2

3.0    PRE-NEGOTIATION                                   4
       3.1  Our Goals                                    4
            3.1.1    Musts
            3.1.2    Trading Cards
            3.1.3    The Bottom Line
       3.2  An Assessment of the Balance of Power        5
            3.2.1    How Much Do We Need Them?
            3.2.2    How Much Do They Need Us?

4.0    THE NEGOTIATIONS                                  7
       4.1  The Resulting Contract                       8

5.0    AN ASSESSMENT OF THE CONTRACT                    12
       5.1  Our Goals Compared with the Results Achieved 12

6.0    RECOMMENDATION                                   15
```

Figure A-7   Table of Contents, British-Style

The Body

The body of the report follows the structure given in the table of contents. Each section's title is placed in a heading with the number and capitalized heading (for example, 4.0 NEGOTIATIONS). Each subsection is placed in a subheading with the first letter of each word capitalized (for example, 4.1 The Resulting Contract). A page format is shown in Figure A-8.

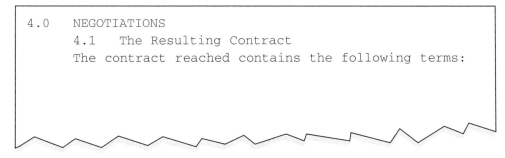

```
4.0    NEGOTIATIONS
       4.1    The Resulting Contract
       The contract reached contains the following terms:
```

Figure A-8 Body of a Report

TONE

Tone is extremely important in negotiation communication. It should be used as a tactical device to create the best atmosphere for negotiations. Tone is definitely a part of strategy since you can either create an atmosphere of mutual benefit (win-win) or confrontation (win-lose). Analyze the three letters presented, especially the underlined sections, to determine both the tone and the strategy (what the writer wishes to achieve) inherent in the tone.

Sensitivity to tone is a must in negotiations. Your tone will be determined by the situation and the strength of your position. Therefore, tone will vary from negotiation to negotiation. However, you must be aware of the tone that you create and how your words will be perceived in order to avoid creating an unintended atmosphere. Certain cultures tend to appear blunt when speaking English, while others appear subservient. Thus, a careful study of tone is essential if you are to avoid communicating false signals. Study the phrases below and then complete the exercise.

1. Use *could, would,* or *might* to make what you communicate seem less blunt.

   That is impossible. *(blunt)*

   That *would* create unnecessary difficulties. *(more diplomatic)*

2. Do not present your ideas as an ultimatum unless you really mean it and have the balance of power strongly in your favor.

   There is no possibility of meeting that deadline. *(ultimatum)*

   We find it difficult to meet the deadline. *(more diplomatic)*

3. Present your ideas more as opinion than fact unless you wish to create a confrontational tone.

   Your figures are wrong. *(blunt)*

   We feel that your figures warrant revision. *(more diplomatic)*

   We wonder where you obtained your figures. *(This raises doubt about the figures in a diplomatic way.)*

4. Avoid using negative words.

> Your attitude is destructive. *(abrasive)*
> We would appreciate greater cooperation. *(more diplomatic)*

5. Present rejections as a result over which you had no control.

> I will not meet your offer. *(blunt)*
> I am afraid that our financial restraints do not allow us to meet
> your offer. *(more diplomatic)*

Note: In rejecting demands, preface your statement by "I / We am/are sorry that"
or "I / We am / are afraid that ..."

6. Use the continuous form with words such as *think, hope, wonder,*
and *plan.* (Only use these words if you have established a very good
working relationship since they might suggest weakness.)

> I think you should accept our offer. *(blunt)*
> I was wondering whether you might accept our offer. *(more diplomatic)*

7. Do not adopt a subservient tone.

> We beg your forgiveness for our failure to meet the deadline.
> *(subservient)*
> Please excuse the delay in our delivery. *(polite, but not subservient)*

8. Try to elicit agreement.

> I think that you will agree that ...

9. Use a question to make a proposal or express an opinion.

> Wouldn't it be better if ...
> Don't you think this would be more appropriate?

10. Use qualifiers such as the following.

> slight disagreement,
> some reservations

11. In stating preferences, use phrases like the following:

> We would rather ...
> We prefer to ...

EXERCISE

Using the examples just discussed or other polite phrases, rewrite the following sentences to make them sound more polite and diplomatic.

1. We cannot do that.
2. I don't want to meet you that early.
3. I want this matter cleared up by Thursday.
4. I cannot accept your offer.
5. We expect you to accept an 8 percent commission.
6. That is your problem, and we have no intention of doing anything about it.
7. Your figures are inaccurate.
8. Your claim for compensation has been rejected.
9. Your offer is an insult.
10. That is a final offer. Take it or leave it.

In addition, learn and use the following phrases in your negotiations.

ELICITING AGREEMENT

Don't you agree that …

POLITE DISAGREEMENT

I'm afraid that I can't agree.

Have you considered that possibly …

On the other hand, …

Don't you see that …

AGREEING

Precisely.

Exactly.

I couldn't agree more.

USING MORE POSITIVE ADJECTIVES TO EXPRESS NEGATIVES

No, not very.

Instead of saying "Their offer was unacceptable," say "The offer was not acceptable."

BALANCING AN ARGUMENT IN ORDER TO EXPRESS NEGATIVES

On the other hand, …

Although you would like … we mustn't forget

GENERALIZING

On the whole, ...

Generally, ...

PRESENTING A COUNTERARGUMENT

I understand your position, but you must consider that ...

APOLOGIZING

Please accept our apologies.

We are sorry to inform you that ...

Unfortunately, ...

STYLE

The discussion of style cannot be as concrete as that of format. The question of style is determined by company policy, as well as personal writing style. To familiarize yourself with the company style, review business documents written in English and talk to the people responsible for typing English correspondence. Secretaries and assistants have a wealth of information just waiting to be tapped.

However, certain generalizations *can* be made about English style that can serve as guidelines. First, English business style is concise. You should be brief and concrete. For example, the French expression *Je vous prie de bien vouloir* is translated *please*. Certain cultures have a tendency to be flowery, even metaphoric, in their writing style. There is little room for poetic devices in English business style. Stick to the facts and keep it brief. Note the following examples of wordiness and suggestions of how to be more concise:

Wordy	Concise
the question as to whether	whether (the question whether)
there is no doubt but that	no doubt (doubtless)
he is a man who	he
in a hasty manner	hastily
this is a subject that	this subject
owing to the fact that	since (Avoid using *the fact that*.)

Politeness and service-mindedness are key elements in English business style. Thus, the use of polite phrases such as *We would appreciate it if*, *at your convenience*, *please consider*, and *thank you for your consideration* is part of good style. The emphasis in this book is on win-win and the creation of a good atmosphere between the negotiators, thus use of the polite phrases is important. Even when expressing a firm stance, you can use phrases that are polite and diplomatic to express your point of view. Learn expressions such as the ones discussed here and get accustomed to using them.

Achieving an Active Style

Verb-Centered Writing

Note how the emphasis on nouns weakens the impact of this sentence.

> The committee made a *recommendation* that there was a *need* for an *improvement* in the company's billing routines.

This verb-centered approach is both more active and more concise.

> The committee *recommended* that the company *improve* its billing routines.

Active versus Passive Voice

In a sentence using active voice, the reader sees immediately who did the action and what the person did because the actor is in the subject's place. When the passive voice is used, the reader must wait until the end of the sentence to see who did the action. Most often the actor might not even be mentioned at all. The active force is stronger.

> *Active voice:* The CEO made the decision.
> *Passive voice:* The decision was made by the CEO.

However, the passive voice can be used when you wish to say what was done without pointing the finger at anyone and is thus considered more diplomatic. It is often used in more formal communication. The passive voice allows you to be more diplomatic and to make your point without embarrassing anyone.

> An excellent opportunity to win the contract was lost.

AN AUDIENCE-CENTERED APPROACH TO WRITING

Remember that you are communicating your ideas to an audience. In order to be effective, you *must* consider your audience's situation and priorities. When communicating, think of it as carrying on a dialogue with your audience. After you have written a couple of sentences, ask yourself, what your audience would say to you after reading those sentences? Their interpretation of these preliminary sentences will influence how they interpret the remainder of your communication. Their response will be *cumulative*—that is, each sentence they read will influence how they interpret the rest of the communication.

The goal of much of your communication will be to get your audience to act in a specific way. To achieve this goal, you must formulate your communication in a way that is attractive to your audience, unless your intention is to be confrontational. However, even in a confrontational communication you can manipulate your audience by creating guilt or a sense of negligence or breach of contract. You must balance your goal of persuading the audience to act in a certain way with a consideration of their situation. Thus, you should provide them with the information they need and show how acting in the desired fashion will benefit them, or in a confrontational letter, how they have no other option.

Appendix 2

TELEPHONE

ENGLISH

The majority of your communication in English will be over the telephone. In fact, in international trade it is possible to have business relationships for years without ever seeing the people with whom you are dealing. It is through the telephone that you project an impression of yourself and the company you represent. Thus, it is extremely important that you master the skills necessary to communicate well over the telephone, which is the purpose of this exercise.

The exercises will make you aware of the subtle differences in communication that make a big difference in the impression you create. Not being aware of these differences can result in your seeming rude, unsophisticated, or even arrogant. It does not take more than saying "I want" instead of "I would like to" to create a bad impression. In addition, there is the cultural element that must be mastered in order to communicate effectively with native English speakers. First, you must be made aware of a standard form, which English telephone conversations often have. So let us take a look at these elements and then practice them until they become second nature

ANSWERING A BUSINESS TELEPHONE CALL

Seven Steps

The following is a list of seven steps you may use to answer the telephone in a business setting.

1. **GREETING**

   Hello

   Good morning

   Good afternoon

The greeting is optional and would be used by switchboard operators (for example, *Good morning, Sun and Fun Tours.*) However, it is appropriate if you are sure the call is coming from outside the company.

2. IDENTIFICATION

Tour Operations, Margaret Smith speaking.

3. OFFER OF HELP

May I help you?

How may I help you?

This is also optional, but recommended when dealing with customers. If you work in customer service, customer relations, or sales, this would be appropriate.

4. EXCHANGE OF INFORMATION

This is the core of the telephone conversation where information is exchanged, requests are made, meetings arranged, and so forth. It is here that you show your sophistication by being informative, polite, and service minded.

5. CONFIRMATION OF MESSAGE

If the caller has made a request, if a meeting date has been set, or if something has been decided, repeat it to be sure that both parties have understood the same thing or that the request is clear. This will help avoid misunderstandings. It is expected as part of a conversation by English-speaking people and makes your telephone manners seem more sophisticated.

6. CONFIRMATION OF ACTION

You confirm that you will do what is requested or what has been decided. If time permits, you should follow this up by confirming your intended action in writing.

7. CLOSING

"Good bye" is standard, but you can make a good final impression in a call by adding something polite or service minded. Consider the following examples:

If you have any other questions, don't hesitate to call.

Thank you for calling. I'm looking forward to our meeting.

EXERCISES

These exercises should be done in pairs. Then some of the pairs will present their conversations in front of the class to be evaluated by their peers on the basis of correctness of English, sophistication of language, and correctness of tone.

1. Arranging a Meeting

Working with a partner use the key phrases and call to arrange a business meeting. Then reverse roles and practice a telephone conversation again.

KEY PHRASES

> Let's set up a meeting.
> When is it convenient for you?
> Wednesday is most convenient for me.
> Let me check my schedule/calendar.
> How about 2:00?   *OR*   Is 2:00 all right/convenient?

2. Informing a Business Associate of an Unfortunate Occurrence

Using the key phrases, call to inform a business associate that you will not be able to live up to an agreement due to some unforeseen events. (For example the failure to meet a deadline is due to the unavailability of raw materials to finish a product, or to a strike which delayed business activity.) Explain the events, their possible impact on the agreement, and what you will try to do to limit their impact.

KEY PHRASES

> I'm afraid that we cannot …
> Unfortunately, …
> We will do our utmost to limit …
> I am sure that we can …
> I'll investigate possible solutions and get back to you.

3. Informing a Business Associate That Your Company Has Accepted the Contract

Using the key phrases, call to inform a business associate that the contract the two of you worked out has been accepted. Arrange to get together to start the implementation process of the business relationship.

KEY PHRASES

> I'm happy/pleased to inform you that ...
> I'm looking forward to a mutually beneficial relationship.
> We are excited about ...
> We want to get moving as soon as possible.
> I would like to visit you as soon as possible to implement the contract.
> When would it be convenient for you?

Appendix 3
NEGOTIATIONS
WORKSHEET

FORMAT OUTLINE

   I. Your Goals (A listing of the priority on the areas to be negotiated.)

     1. Decide on the *musts* (high-priority items) and if there is any room for negotiation concerning them.

     2. Set bottom lines for those items which are negotiable.

     3. Decide on "trading cards," if any, and what you expect to get in return.

     4. Generally decide what you expect to get in return for any concessions you make.

     5. Set a bottom line for the contract as a whole.

  II. An Assessment of the Balance of Power

    A. Evaluate what the other side stands to gain by this association and what you stand to gain. Make a fair evaluation, otherwise this will only lead to a false sense of power.

     1. Evaluate what you can offer them in this deal, what they can offer you, and who needs whom the most.

    B. Decide what you can say or do in the negotiations to impress on the other side your position of power (remembering all the time that you are walking a fine line between trying to attain your goals as nearly as possible while still reaching a mutually satisfying agreement).

 III. Determination of Your Strategy Based on I and II

    A. Determine your opening stance, and make a summary of your opening statement.

     1. Is your position going to be flexible or hard-line?

     2. Do you have the power to enforce your position?

    B. Are you going to negotiate the *musts* or the medium- and low-priority items first?

    C. Are you going to set any pre-conditions? (Careful with this one!!)

NEGOTIATIONS WORKSHEET FILL-IN

I. YOUR GOALS

    A. Our priority(ies) is/are

    B. Our bottom line on this/these is/are

    C. To achieve our priority(ies) we are willing to use item(s)
        number _____ as our trading cards.

    D. We are willing to concede (what?)

        (How much—if the trading card is quantifiable?)

        (What item and/or aspect of an item if the trading card is not quantifiable?)

    E. Our bottom line (what we have to obtain for the total contract) is

II. AN ASSESSMENT OF THE BALANCE OF POWER

    A. Why are we entering into negotiations?

        What do we stand to gain?

        How will our situation be improved?

        How much do we need them?

        What alternatives do we have, and at what point should we
        walk away from negotiations?

B. Why is the other side entering into negotiations?

What do they stand to gain?

How will their situation be improved?

How much do they need us?

What alternatives do they have, and at what point will they probably walk away from negotiations? (Here you will have to make an educated guess)

III. DETERMINATION OF YOUR STRATEGY BASED ON I AND II
   A. Our opening stance will be

   1. We will create this stance by the following opening statement:

   B. We will push to negotiate the following item first:

   C. If we get what we want on the first item, how will we treat the other items on the agenda?

   D. Will we set any pre-conditions? (This is usually not wise if you don't have the balance of power in your favor.)

Appendix 4
POSITION
PRESENTATION
WORKSHEET

FORMAT OUTLINE

In Chapter 1, "The Art of Negotiating," you learned that a well-documented position is one of the most effective means of convincing your counterparts of the fairness of your own position. Thus, in advance of all negotiations, you will fill out a Presentation of Position Worksheet for all of your major positions including the following:

1. A statement of your position

2. Factual support of your position, including the source of your facts

3. Consequences of the rejection by the other side of your position. This can include a hint of your willingness to negotiate on a point, which will be inherent in the language you use in describing the consequences. For example, using "possible deficits" suggests some flexibility, whereas "negative cash flow" reflects a more inflexible position.

4. Their counterargument—what you expect them to argue against your position

5. Your arguments to meet their counterargument

The example is from Case 6: "Tourism Comes to Zanir." It provides you with a model when filling out your Position Presentation Worksheet.

1. POSITION: We require 51 percent ownership of the project including the cost of the hotel stay. Thus, we require that you break down the cost of the package sold in your country and transfer 51 percent of the cost of the hotel stay to us in German marks. The calculation of the hotel stay will be determined by agreement between your accountant and ours.

2. DOCUMENTATION: Our neighboring country developed a similar resort project to that which you propose, based on 100 percent ownership of the resort by the foreign company. Their experience shows that 90 percent of the money spent by tourists was either spent in buying the package in the company's country or spent at the hotel. Thus, the revenues generated in the host country, DM 1,000,000 per year, were not sufficient to cover the costs of improving the infrastructure necessary for the project. Here are the figures furnished by the Sendalian Ministry of Commerce for your review.

3. CONSEQUENCES: Based on these figures, the project would result in negative cash flow for our country. You must admit that for a project to be attractive, there has to be a profit potential in it for both sides. (Note the appeal to fairness and commonly accepted good business practices.)

4. THEIR COUNTERARGUMENT: We will be providing jobs and training and upgrading the infrastructure, which will allow for further development of the tourist industry, all of which will help you generate revenue.

5. YOUR COUNTERARGUMENT: Nevertheless, we have estimated that the increased revenues due to new jobs and training will be DM _____ which will hardly be sufficient to cover our estimated costs of DM _____.

POSITION PRESENTATION WORKSHEET FILL-IN

1. Your position on the first item to be negotiated is

2. Documentation
    Statistics

    Other similar cases and the conditions and agreements reached
    (Appealing to objective criteria)

    Other alternatives (If you have some other alternatives, you can
    use them to justify your demands.)

3. Consequences of your not getting all that you asked for
    How willing are you to compromise and how far are you willing to go?
    (This should be prepared in advance, but not told to the other side)

4. Their counterargument will probably be

5. Your argument to meet their counterargument will be

Appendix 5

A COMPILATION

OF LANGUAGE EXERCISES

USING POLITE, DIPLOMATIC, AND STRATEGIC LANGUAGE

All cases will require the use of polite, diplomatic, and strategic language. In each case you will be referred to this section. Practice these expressions until they become second nature.

Could, would, please, and *appreciate*

Using these expressions creates a much more polite tone and a sense of respect. Compare the following:

Do it.	We *would* appreciate your doing it
We want the meeting on ...	*Could* we meet on ... ?

CHECKING THAT YOU HAVE UNDERSTOOD/ASKING FOR CLARIFICATION

Please correct me if I'm wrong, but ...

Could I ask a few questions to see whether I have understood your position?

As I understand it ...

Let's sum up then. You propose ...

Could we go through that again?

Could you explain that point again?

I am not sure that I understand your position. Do you mean that ... ?

SHOWING WILLINGNESS TO COOPERATE

We would like to settle this issue in a mutually satisfactory way.

We'd be happy to settle this point in a mutually cooperative way.

SHOWING UNDERSTANDING OF YOUR COUNTERPARTS' POSITION

We appreciate your problem, but …

We can understand your difficulty, but …

FOCUSING ON DIFFICULTIES

The main problem as we see it is …

Where we have difficulty with your proposal is …

REJECTING AN OFFER

I'm afraid we won't be able to accept that. (*diplomatic*)

I'm afraid that you are going to have to meet our requests on this item if we are going to reach an agreement.

That is totally out of the question. (*strong*)

ACCEPTING AN OFFER

I think we can accept that.

I think we can agree on that.

EXERCISE

In pairs, test your mastery of the phrases presented so far. Student A will ask Student B, "Give me a phrase using *could* or *would.*" After Student B has responded, he or she will then ask Student A to give a phrase checking understanding or showing willingness to cooperate. Continue until all sections have been covered.

Expressing Opinions

PRESENTING AN OPINION

It seems to me … / It appears to me … *(weak)*

I feel that… / I think that… / It is my opinion that … *(neutral)*

I am convinced that… / I strongly/firmly believe that …*(strong)*

There is no question/doubt that. … *(very strong)*

As I see it …

My understanding is …

PRESENTING AN OPINION CONTRARY TO ONE THAT HAS BEEN STATED

> I can't agree with …
> My understanding is …
> I am not so sure about that …
> As I see it …
> Wait a minute, do you really feel that … ?
> I feel …

GETTING ANOTHER PERSON'S OPINION

> Mr. Smith, I would like your opinion/input on this matter.
> Mr. Smith, what do you think/feel about this matter?

Agreeing and Disagreeing

AGREEING

> I generally agree. *(agreement with reservation) (This is usually followed by an explanation of what reservations the speaker has and why.)*
> I agree. *(neutral)*
> I fully/completely agree. *(strong)*

DISAGREEING

> I'm afraid that I cannot agree because … *(polite disagreement with an explanation of why)*
> I can see your point, but … *(polite disagreement)*
> I cannot totally agree. My problem is … *(partial disagreement followed by a statement of where and why the speaker disagrees)*
> I cannot completely agree. *(partial disagreement)*
> I strongly/totally disagree. *(strong)*
> I'm afraid I see some negative consequences of X's opinion which are …*(disagreeing and making a case for one's opinion)*

EXERCISE

Work in groups of four to five students to complete this exercise. One student should express an opinion and then, using the phrases presented above, the other students should in turn express agreement or disagreement and state why. After two students have expressed an opinion, the remaining ones can choose to agree or disagree with any of the previously stated opinions. After three or four students have expressed their reaction to the original opinion or any of the other students' responses, a new student will express a new opinion and the other students will respond.

TACTICAL DISAGREEMENT

I wonder if we would be best served by …

(This phrase suggests that the present proposal will not help to reach a goal and that the speaker's proposal will. It is formulated to suggest that both sides would profit by accepting the speaker's proposal, and it places the proposal in a positive light.)

Wouldn't it be better to/if we … *(The effect is similar to that of the previous phrase.)*

I suggest a compromise that will serve both sides' interests. *(This creates a feeling of mutuality while rejecting the present proposal.)*

Let us say that if we were both to give a little and agree on 6 1/2 percent … *(This statement creates the same feeling as the previous sentence , but gives particulars.)*

EXERCISE

In pairs consisting of one member from each negotiating team, practice responding to proposals relevant to the case you are working on. Use the four alternatives mentioned or similar ones that you develop.

Proposals and Counterproposals

MAKING PROPOSALS

Making proposals should include not only the proposal, but the rationale behind the proposal. Thus, use expressions such as the following:

We offer our agents a 6 percent commission. / Our company policy is a 6 percent commission.

(This suggests a firm position with little leeway for discussion unless the counterpart has very good reasons for an exception.)

We propose a 6 percent commission, which is standard in the industry.
(This suggests a strong position based on common practice, but does leave leeway for discussion.)

We suggest a 6 percent commission since this is standard in the industry.
(This suggests a greater flexibility than the two previous statements.)

MAKING COUNTERPROPOSALS

We understand your proposal, but due to ... we feel that 7 percent would be a fair figure.

> *(This shows that you have listened to your counterpart's proposal, but due to certain reasons, 7 percent is fair—note the appeal to fairness.)*

Considering ... (name special conditions), don't you feel that 7 percent would be fairer?

> *(Note how the speaker puts her or his counterpart in the position of agreeing or seeming unfair.)*

I'm afraid that we cannot accept less than 7 percent because ... / due to ...

We feel that due to/because of ..., that 7 percent would be justified, but we are willing to meet you half way at 6 1/2 percent.

> *(Note how the speaker appeals to fairness by using "justified," based on the root "just" meaning "fair," while at the same time showing flexibility.)*

EXERCISE

In pairs consisting of one member from each negotiating team, practice making proposals and counterproposals. Remember to support your statements with facts and reasons.

CALLING A COUNTERPART'S STATEMENTS/FACTS INTO DOUBT

Your counterparts will often make claims that favor their position. You must not allow these claims to go unchallenged since they can be half-truths based on a limited sampling, or merely opinion. In the following exercise Student A will make a claim, Student B will call it into doubt, Student A will try to substantiate the claim, and then Student B will question that claim or offer a different set of facts which he or she will have to substantiate. Use the following expressions to question the claims.

I would like to see the source of your figures.
Excuse me, but what is the source of your statistics/facts?
Excuse me, but can I see the material on which your claims are based?
I am afraid that your statistics tell only half of the story.

> *(Go on to explain why the statistics are incomplete—for example the base year chosen was favorable to Student A's position, or that there may be reasons for the result other than those that Student A would like you to believe. Concerning the latter, management might claim that productivity has stagnated and workers do not deserve a raise, while leaving out that the old and malfunctioning machinery is really the cause of the low productivity and not the workers' efforts.)*

Let's look at the real factors behind your statistics.

(Go on to explain the other half of the truth that Student A has purposely left out.)

I am afraid I don't follow your argument. Could you explain it more clearly?

(Use this when Student A's argument is obviously false. Let Student A get tied up in his or her own faulty argument.)

Are you sure about those figures? Ours show that … and our source is very credible.

EXERCISE

Student A: Make a claim involving some type of support. For example:

"You are demanding a 10 percent raise, which will put you 5 percent above the national average at the same time that productivity has declined by 3 percent over the last year."

Student B: Question that claim. Say the following or something similar:

"I would like to see the source of your figures about the national average for our industry's workers. Furthermore, productivity declines can be blamed on malfunctioning machinery, which we have pointed out to management several times."

Student A:

"Our source is the National Association of Manufacturers."

Student B:

"That's strange, because our source is the National Bureau of Labor Statistics, which is the most reliable source of labor statistics. Maybe we should trust them."

Go through this process concerning at least four claims relevant to the case you are working on.

ESTABLISHING TONE

Opening statements will establish the tone of the negotiations. Practice opening statements to create the following tones:

collaborative	businesslike but pleasant
combative	firm
formal	flattering
informal	

EXERCISE

Before making the presentation relevant to a case, carefully choose words to convey the proper tone. Work in pairs and make a presentation to your partner relevant to a case. Get her or his response to your presentation to see if your partner perceived the intended tone. Have her or him state which words conveyed the tone that was perceived. If necessary, make the presentation twice to give your partner the chance to note the key words. You can combine several tones such as flattering, formal, and collaborative. Have your partner determine which words or phrases conveyed which tone.

AVOIDING LOCKED-IN POSITIONS BY EXPLORING ALTERNATIVES

One of the common mistakes made by negotiators is that they lock themselves into a predetermined position. One of the basic notions behind principled negotiation is the idea that in most negotiations, predetermined, locked-in positions are counterproductive. Thus, you, as a sensitive negotiator, must be sensitive to your counterparts' interests and try to find a common ground, which can often involve finding alternative solutions. Consider, for example, the case of two students in a hot library room. One has a cold and wants the window closed and the other is sweating and wants the window open. Focusing on the open or closed window will get them nowhere, but focusing on interests will allow them to arrive at an alternative solution. One student wants to cool the room down while the other wants to avoid a draft. Thus, an alternate solution might be to open a window in another room, allowing the heat to escape while not causing a draft.

EXERCISE

In pairs, define a situation where it would be easy to lock yourselves into a fixed position. Defined the fixed positions (for example: window open versus window closed), then look for alternative solutions by trying to find common interests, using one of the phrases below followed by a proposal of an alternative that will satisfy the needs of both parties.

> We haven't considered a third possibility.
> What if we … *(then suggest a third possibility)*
> We should not limit ourselves. What if we could expand the pie by …
> We could satisfy both our interests by …
> We should explore an alternative solution. What if …
> You know we haven't considered …

There's no use arguing from locked-in positions. Let's look for a common ground. What are your primary interests?

(You may or may not get your counterpart to disclose these interests, but if you do, you should disclose yours too. Otherwise it will be seen as a tactical maneuver. Once you use an appeal to find a common ground as a tactical maneuver, you will destroy the trust necessary to arrive at a common ground solution or perhaps any solution).

INTERPRETING HIDDEN MEANING

Negotiators often will not commit themselves because they don't want to lock themselves into a position. They wish to leave the backdoor open for escape and to save face. Thus, they often will use vague, but significant expressions. The counterparts must be sensitive to reading between the lines.

EXERCISE

Analyze the following statements and interpret what the speaker might have been implying.

At the present time, we are not prepared to expand our production and take on new employees.

We don't normally do that.

We can agree on the general outline of the agenda.

We are presently satisfied with our supplier.

Working in pairs, make general statements and interpret what hidden meaning they may contain. Student A should make a general statement which suggests a hidden meaning. Student B should guess at the hidden meaning and make an appropriate comment. For example, in response to the first statement, Student B might say: "However, in six months if we were to do ... would you consider taking on new employees?"

Making Negative Statements into More Positive Ones

SOFTENING CONFRONTATIONAL STATEMENTS

In dealing with cultures that avoid confrontation, phrasing of your position is extremely important. Compare "This is our final offer" with "I question whether we have leeway to stretch our offer much further." The first is confrontational, while the second allows the other team to meet you by proposing a counteroffer.

Working in pairs, read the following confrontational statements and rephrase them so they sound more diplomatic.

1. Your unyielding position is creating an impossible atmosphere.
2. There is no way that we can meet your demands.
3. This is the best offer you are going to get.
4. You are lying and we know it.
5. Your figures are false.
6. If you are not willing to make a reasonable offer, we can break off negotiations right now.
7. So far you have been unwilling to compromise.
8. You do not appreciate our situation.
9. Are you willing to accept our offer or not?
10. Do you really think yours is a fair offer?
11. We do not want to go out socializing with you.

TURNING NEGATIVE STATEMENTS INTO MORE POSITIVE ONES

Compare the following statements:

1. This is impossible.
2. There would be a greater possibility for success if …

The first sentence sounds confrontational. It probably would close the door to discussion and get you nowhere. The second statement, on the other hand, takes a positive approach. It suggests the possibility of success and introduces the conditions necessary to achieve that success.

Working in pairs, read the following negative statements and turn them into positive ones. Do not use words with prefixes such as *un-*, *il-*, *dis-*, and so forth.

1. You are being uncooperative.
2. Reaching agreement seems unlikely.
3. Your position remains unchanged and you seem inflexible.
4. Our present line of discussion is unproductive.
5. Your proposal is uninteresting.
6. Your perception of the situation is one-sided.
7. We are very dissatisfied with your initial offer.
8. Why are you so unwilling to meet us half way?

Index